CW01209124

CONTENTS

THE EARTH IS ALIVE!	4
IN THE BEGINNING	6
JOURNEY TO THE CENTRE OF THE EARTH	8
DRIFT	12
FAULTS AND FOLDS	14
BRACE FOR IMPACT!	16
VOLCANOES	18
HOW IS A VOLCANO STRUCTURED?	20
A WIDE RANGE	22
VOLCANO MAP	26
ERUPTIONS	28
TYPES OF ERUPTIONS	30
EACH ONE UNIQUE	32
A DANGEROUS ARSENAL	34
A BRIEF HISTORY OF VOLCANOES	38
ERUPTIONS TO REMEMBER!	38
VOLCANOES TODAY	42
BEYOND FIRE	46
EARTHQUAKES	46
TSUNAMIS	48
ASH CLOUDS	50
MUDFLOWS	50
CALDERAS, GEYSERS AND MORE!	52
CALDERAS	52
SECONDARY VOLCANISM	54
GEYSERS	55
STUDYING VOLCANOES	56
A VOLCANO IN THE NEIGHBOURHOOD	58
IT'S YOUR TURN!	60

WHY DO VOLCANOES EXIST ON EARTH?

Our planet is dotted with volcanoes. Some are extinct and others are active. Each volcanoe is unique, but all of them allow us to see what is happening inside the Earth and to learn about the primordial forces that shaped our planet and still wield an effect on it today. The Earth emits enormous amounts of energy through volcanoes.

This map shows some of the most famous and powerful volcanoes.

Take a journey to these mountains of fire and learn all about them.

- Mount Rainier
- Eyjafjallajökul
- Mount Saint Helens
- San Andreas Fault
- Kīlauea
- Mauna Kea
- Mauna Loa
- Popocatépetl
- Teide
- Galeras
- Osorno

2

Ključevskaja Sopka

Vesuvius

Etna

Changbaishan

Mount Fuji

Nyiragongo

Rift Valley

Pinatubo

Ol Doinyo Lengai

Merapi

Kelimutu

Whakaari

Mount Erebus

THE EARTH IS ALIVE!

THE EARTH'S CREATION
Our planet is billions of years old and has undergone lots of changes over time. And it's still changing today.

CONTINENTAL DRIFT AND TECTONIC PLATES
The continents didn't always look the way they do today. They've shifted plenty over the years.

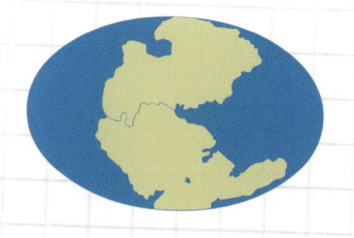

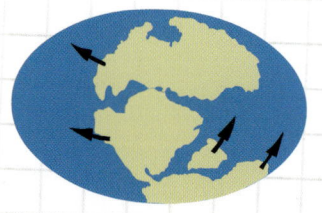

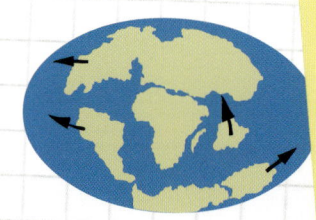

LAND OF FIRE
As the **continents shift**, they sometimes bang into each other forcefully, creating a series of very warm areas where most volcanoes are located.

Our planet may seem like a solid and unchanging mass, but appearances can be deceiving. Under our feet, far below the surface, the Earth is constantly mutating. Much of this activity is imperceptible to us, but every once in a while, it makes itself felt loud and clear, through phenomena as spectacular as they are dangerous: eruptions.

Though we can predict these eruptions and scientists all over the world monitor them, there is also still much to learn about them! To understand eruptions and volcanoes, first you have to understand the makeup of the Earth. You'll learn all about it in this book.

VOLCANOES

Volcanic eruptions are amazing natural sights! Each is unpredictable and unique, which is why there is still so much to learn about them.

EARTHQUAKES AND OTHER NATURAL DISASTERS

But while eruptions are incredible to witness, they are also dangerous, and unfortunately, they are often accompanied by other natural disasters, such as **earthquakes** and **tidal waves**. But we have learned to live alongside these ticking time bombs.

IN THE BEGINNING

To understand our planet, you have to know how it all started. The Earth dates back billions of years, and it has a very turbulent history!

1) WHEN DID THE EARTH FORM?

Our planet formed about **4.6 billion years ago**, and the solar system formed at the same time. All the major planets in our solar system came from the same **solar nebula**, a giant cloud of gas and dust that, like an enormous centrifuge, revolved around the centre, which became the sun.

2) HOW DID IT FORM?

Inside the solar nebula, the Earth and other planets began to take shape. Bits of dust and metal and other matter began to unite to form minuscule **celestial bodies**, including chunks that would become the Earth. Gravity caused these disparate masses to continue to join together, and they grew larger and larger. One of these large masses was the Earth.

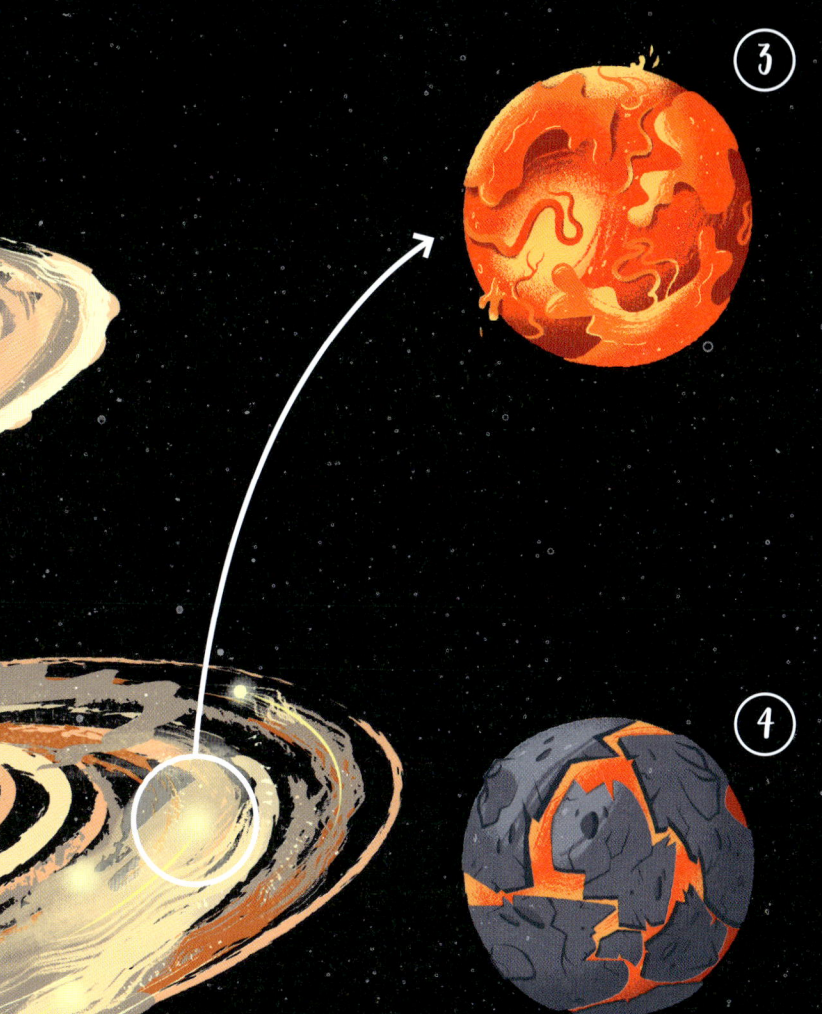

③ HOW DID IT GET ITS SHAPE?

All this energy raised the temperature of the newly formed Earth, causing **fusion**! The denser metals were pulled to the core, while the lighter metals were distributed to the middle layer and the lightest metals of all ended up on the surface of this very hot sphere.

④ WHY DID IT BECOME SOLID?

At this point the Earth was a large incandescent mass. The very high temperatures helped form a thick gas cloud that cooled it down. A **solid crus**t formed and then gradually became thicker and formed the continents.

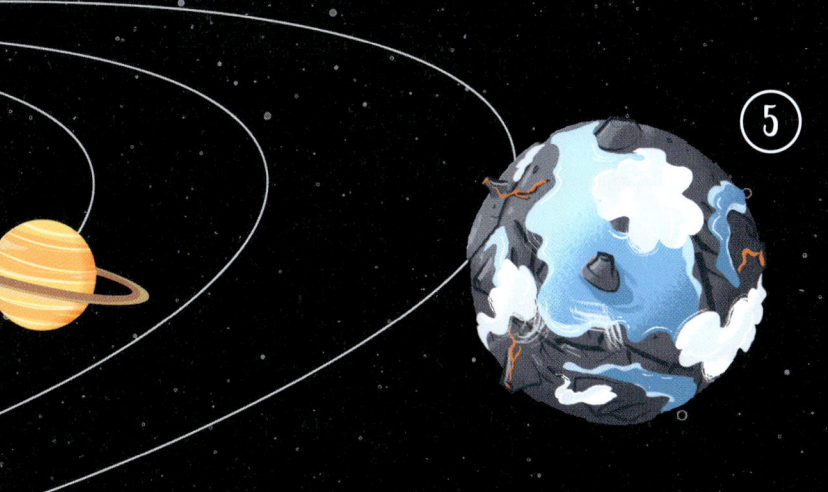

⑤ HOW WERE THE OCEANS FORMED?

At the same time, the atmosphere was changing rapidly. The cooling of the Earth's surface created a large amount of water vapor, mixed with various gases. This caused rain to fall, and eventually the rain collected in enormous puddles of water in large hollows in the Earth's crust. These were the **primordial oceans**!

7

JOURNEY TO THE CENTRE OF THE EARTH

The Earth is formed of various layers, much like an onion. The layers run more than 6,000 kilometres (3,730 miles) below the surface and reach extremely high temperatures! Let's take a look at the Earth, beginning with the outer layer, the 'onionskin'.

CRUST

WHAT IS THE EARTH'S SURFACE?
The **crust** is 7 to 50 kilometres (4.3 to 31 miles) thick. It's thinner below the oceans and thicker below the continents.

50 km (31 miles)
7 km (4.3 miles)

DID YOU KNOW...?
Man has travelled into space but has never gone to the centre of the Earth! The **deepest hole** in the Earth, drilled in Russia, went only 12 kilometres (7.5 miles) deep.

8

WHAT IS THE MANTLE?

The mantle is the layer just below the crust that is up to 2,900 kilometres (1,800 miles) thick. It is dense and very hot—so hot that molten rock turns into thick **magma** that moves very slowly.

MANTLE

OUTER CORE

INNER CORE

Magma is extremely hot liquid or semi-liquid rock mixed with dissolved gases and other liquids.

WHAT IS IN THE EARTH'S CORE?

The **core**, located below the mantle, is the innermost part of the planet. It is more than 5,000 kilometres (3,100 miles) below the surface, and its internal temperature is extremely hot—it can reach 5000°C (9000°F).

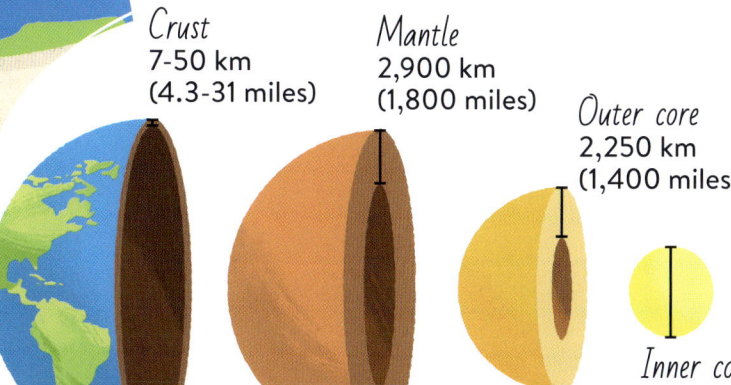

Crust
7-50 km
(4.3-31 miles)

Mantle
2,900 km
(1,800 miles)

Outer core
2,250 km
(1,400 miles)

Inner core
1,300 km
(810 miles)

The Earth's core is divided into two parts: the outer core, which is made up of liquid, and the inner core, which is solid and made up largely of iron and nickel. The inner core is the true centre of the Earth!

9

The image on the previous page is a simplified version of the Earth's structure. In reality it's much more complex. Let's take a closer look.

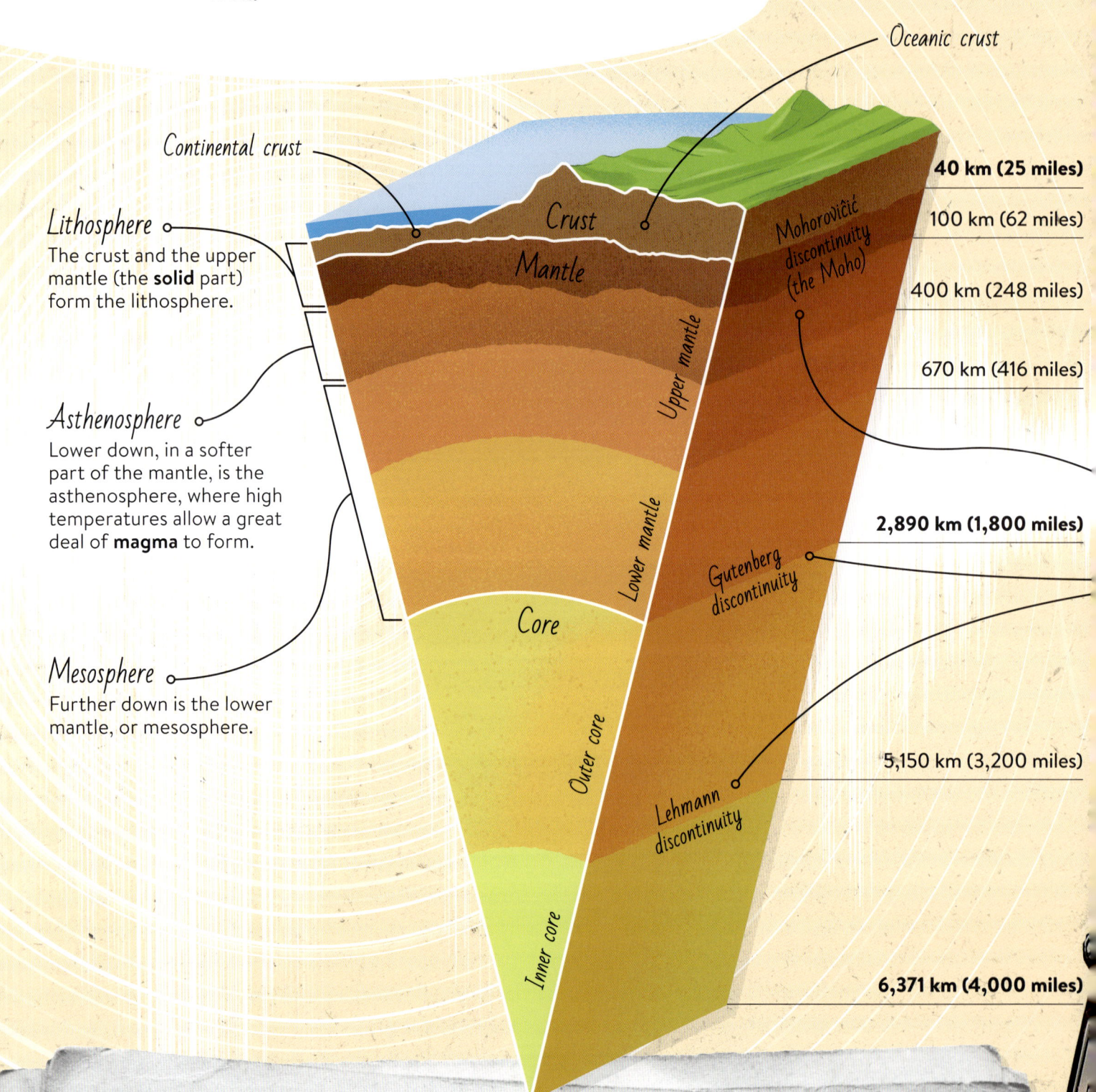

Oceanic crust

Continental crust

40 km (25 miles)

Lithosphere
The crust and the upper mantle (the **solid** part) form the lithosphere.

Crust

Mantle

Mohorovičić discontinuity (the Moho)

100 km (62 miles)

400 km (248 miles)

Upper mantle

670 km (416 miles)

Asthenosphere
Lower down, in a softer part of the mantle, is the asthenosphere, where high temperatures allow a great deal of **magma** to form.

Lower mantle

2,890 km (1,800 miles)

Gutenberg discontinuity

Core

Mesosphere
Further down is the lower mantle, or mesosphere.

Outer core

5,150 km (3,200 miles)

Lehmann discontinuity

Inner core

6,371 km (4,000 miles)

HOW IS THE EARTH'S STRUCTURE STUDIED?
Most of the work of studying the structure of the Earth is performed using **seismic waves**, the same kind of vibrations we feel when there is an earthquake. Since we haven't yet figured out how to travel into the depths of the Earth, they are a very important analytical tool!

Dilation — Compression

Wavelength

Longitudinal P waves

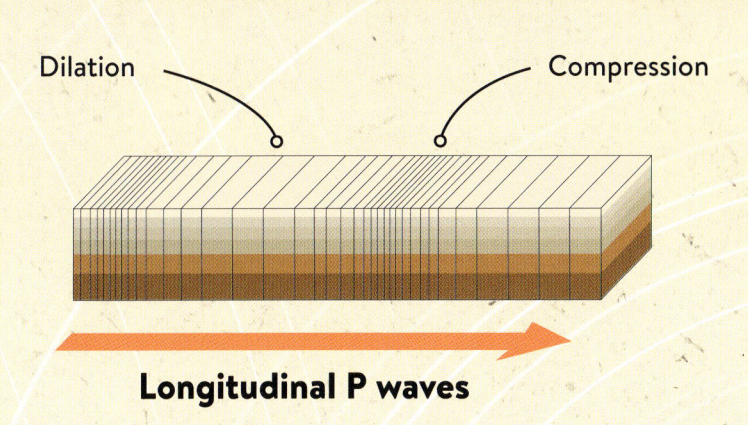

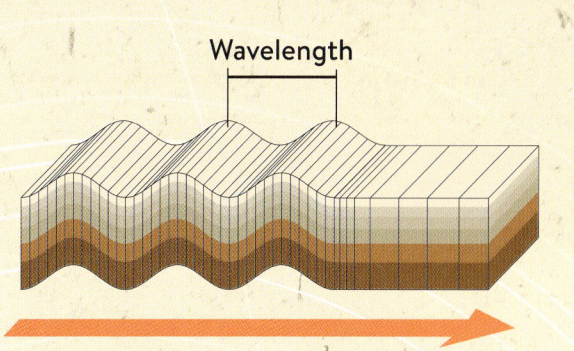

Transverse S waves

WHAT'S THE DIFFERENCE BETWEEN P WAVES AND S WAVES?
Not all seismic waves are the same. P waves (also called **longitudinal** or **compressional waves**) are faster and can occur in both liquids and solids. S waves (also called **transverse waves**) are slower and occur only in solids. By recording the movement of these waves in the Earth and their varying speeds, geologists learn about the structure of the planet!

WHAT ARE SEISMIC DISCONTINUITIES?
Seismic discontinuities are areas where P waves increase in velocity. There are three of these areas: between the crust and the upper mantle, between the mantle and the core and between the outer and inner core. They were named for the scientists who discovered them from the late 1800s to the mid-1900s: Andrija Mohorovičić, Beno Gutenberg and Inge Lehmann.

DID YOU KNOW...?
Long before modern science began to explain the Earth's core, writer **Jules Verne** imagined the depths of the Earth in his novel *Journey to the Centre of the Earth*, published in 1864. While the book is pure fantasy, a lot of what Verne imagined is based on theories from that era.

DRIFT

The Earth's surface did not always look as it does today. Over millions of years, oceans have formed and vanished, mountain ranges have formed and entire continents have moved. Let's learn how it all happened!

WHAT IS THE LITHOSPHERE?

The lithosphere is like a jigsaw puzzle made of different pieces, or **plates**, that are constantly moving over the Earth's surface. They're even moving right now, but the movements are imperceptible!

HOW DO THE PLATES MOVE?

The plates are pushed by the internal forces of the planet. They move by almost floating atop the magma in the asthenosphere and can drift from 2 to 20 centimetres (3/4 inch to 8 inches) per year. The plates move independently of one another and drag land (if they are **continental plates**) or ocean (if they are **oceanic plates**) or both with them.

WHO WAS ALFRED WEGENER?

Alfred Wegener was a German scientist who in 1915 presented a new theory about **continental drift**. He theorised that the current arrangement of the continents is the result of fragmentation of a supercontinent called **Pangaea** during the prehistoric era. He believed North America detached from Europe, and South America from Africa, allowing the Atlantic Ocean to be created. Other movements then created the Earth's mountain ranges. That explained how certain species could be found on different continents. Wegener's theory would not become widely accepted until the 1960s!

DID YOU KNOW...?

As far as we know, Earth is the only planet where this kind of movement happens! The **theory of plate tectonics** was developed by J. T. Wilson in the 1960s.

DO THE PLATES MOVE IN A SPECIFIC DIRECTION?

Scientists are still studying which direction the plates move. Many scholars believe that they travel along convection currents produced by heat from the mantle, meaning they follow the path that magma travels as it moves.

There are about a dozen tectonic plates. The main ones are:

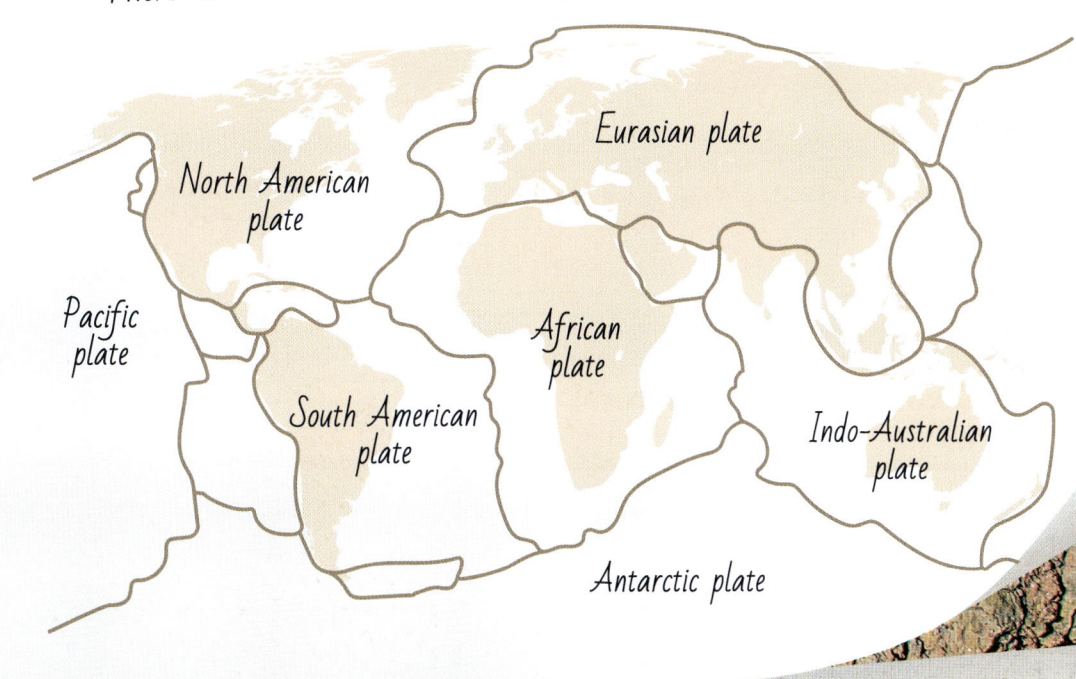

- North American plate
- Eurasian plate
- Pacific plate
- African plate
- South American plate
- Indo-Australian plate
- Antarctic plate

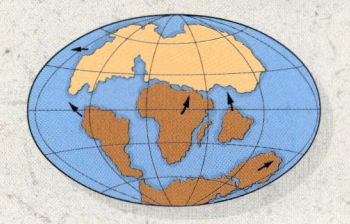

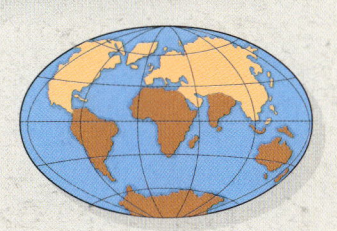

Approximately 225 million years ago
The supercontinent Pangaea surrounded by the Panthalassic Ocean.

Approximately 150 million years ago
Pangaea splits into Laurasia and Gondwana.

Approximately 100 million years ago
The continents begin to form.

Today
The continents today.

FAULTS AND FOLDS

Because the plates move independently of each other, they can collide, giving rise to various phenomena.

A RIFT AMIDST THE GLACIERS
The **Silfra fissure**, in Iceland, is located on the border between the North American plate and the Eurasian plate.

Silfra, Iceland

WHAT'S THE MOST FAMOUS FAULT ON THE PLANET?
The **San Andreas fault**, in California. It's 1,200 kilometres (750 miles) long and runs along the boundary between the North American and Pacific plates.

WHAT ARE FAULTS?
Faults are very deep cracks in the land created when two plates move at different velocities. As they slide against each other, tension in the rock below can cause an earthquake.

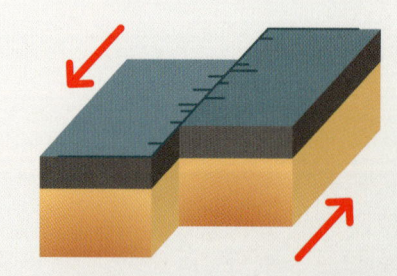

WHY ARE THE OCEANS GROWING?

The crust underneath the oceans is thinner than the continental crust. When two plates in the oceanic crust separate, magma can rise up. Once the magma cools, it becomes part of the ocean floor, which means the area of the ocean grows larger. The Pacific Ocean is growing the most quickly—20 centimetres (8 inches) per year!

SEA OR OCEAN?

The **Red Sea**, in Egypt, is a fascinating example of a sea that is expanding. Though the terminology is still under debate, it seems destined to become the planet's sixth ocean!

Red Sea

ARE THERE MOUNTAINS UNDERWATER?

Yes. The **mid-ocean ridge** is the longest mountain chain on Earth! It winds around the borders of plates all over the ocean floor and is an astonishing 65,000 kilometres (40,390 miles) long. It includes valleys and trenches, such as the **Mariana trench**, the deepest point in the world!

Mariana Trench

BRACE FOR IMPACT!

When two plates collide, the effects can be amazing—and even explosive. Depending on the types of plates involved, there can be earthquakes and eruptions. These phenomena don't occur in random places, but in very specific spots.

WHAT IS A SUBDUCTION ZONE?

A subduction zone is a spot where **plates collide**, causing the Earth to shake and volcanoes to erupt. Typically, one of the two plates slides underneath the other toward the asthenosphere and turns into magma.

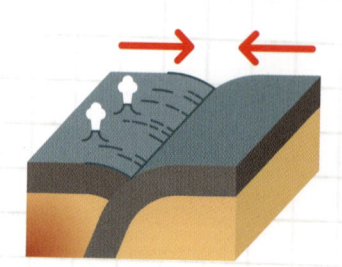

WHAT HAPPENS AFTER PLATES COLLIDE?

That all depends on what types of plates collide. The **thickness** of the plates involved is key. One plate slides under the other, and if heat and pressure rise to extreme levels, **magma** is pushed upward and erupts above the surface.

WHAT ARE THE DIFFERENT RESULTS?

Continental crust against continental crust
In this case, when one plate slides below the other, the collision is strong enough to create entire mountain ranges. That's how the Alps and the Himalayas were formed.

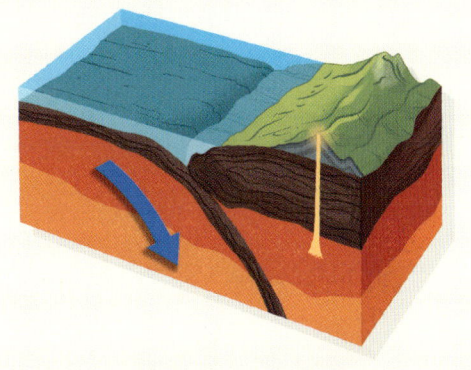

Oceanic crust against continental crust
When two different types of crust collide, the thinner one (the oceanic crust) slides below the thicker one (the continental crust) and magma erupts and gradually forms a series of volcanoes.

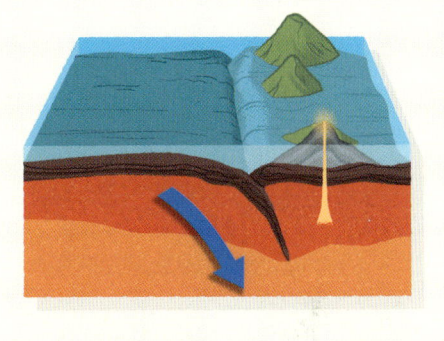

Oceanic crust against oceanic crust
When two thin pieces of oceanic crust collide and one slides under the other, magma erupts, and an arc of volcanic islands is formed.

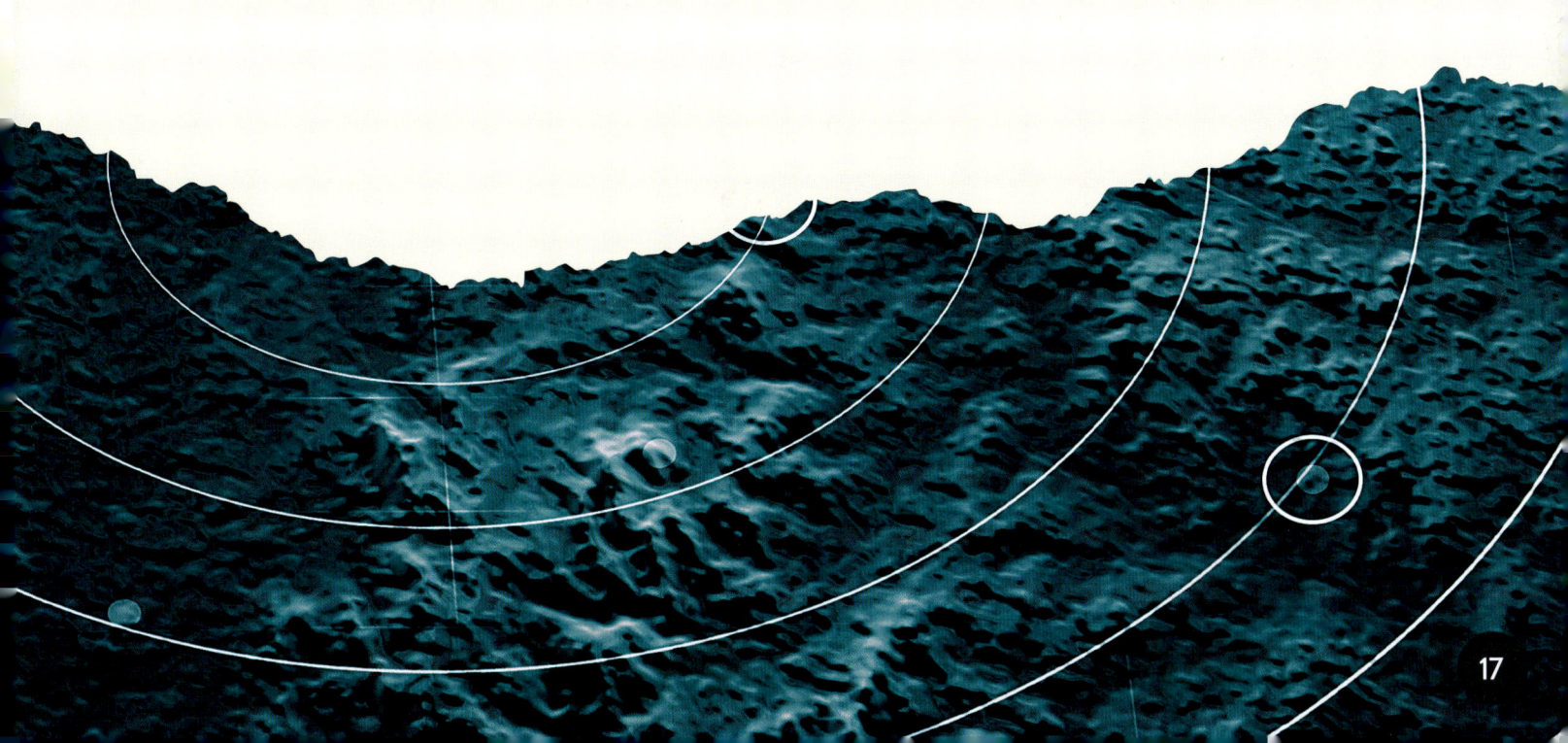

17

VOLCANOES

1,500

35 years

HOW MANY VOLCANOES ARE THERE IN THE WORLD TODAY?

There are about 1,500, if you count only those that have erupted during human history, meaning those that are active or potentially active.

WHAT'S THE MOST ACTIVE VOLCANO ON EARTH?

Kīlauea, in Hawaii, is the most active volcano by any measure. The longest eruption ever recorded was Kilauea. This eruption lasted 35 years, from 1983 to 2018! In 2020, it began erupting once more.

VOLCANOES CAN BE:

active
A volcano that has erupted at least once in the last 10,000 years.

dormant
A volcano for which little activity has been recorded in the last 10,000 years is considered to be at rest.

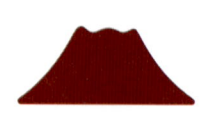

extinct
A volcano that has not exhibited any type of activity in the last 10,000 years.

What, exactly, are volcanoes? They are rifts in the Earth's crust where magma, ash and gas escape. When we think of volcanoes, most often we picture perfectly conical mountains, but there are lots of different types. Let's take a look at the form these fiery giants can take!

DID YOU KNOW...?
The **Greek island Santorini**, known for its charming white and blue villages, isn't actually an island at all—it's a volcano! It is the eastern side of a large dormant crater that recently has shown signs of becoming active.

WHERE DOES THE WORD 'VOLCANO' COME FROM?
The word 'volcano' comes from the name of the ancient Roman god of fire: **Vulcan**, also the **god of metalworking and the forge**. According to Greco-Roman myth, Vulcan forged beautiful swords and ornaments, in contrast with his own ugly looks, in a foundry located beneath Etna.

19

HOW IS A VOLCANO STRUCTURED?

There are different kinds of volcanoes, but almost all of them have three basic elements: the crater, the vent and the magma chamber. Let's take a closer look!

MAIN VENT
The **main vent** is a cavity that is usually long and narrow. The magma rises through it to the surface.

MAGMA CHAMBER
The magma chamber is the spot where the magma from the mantle collects. It is located below the volcano in the Earth's crust, 3 to 4 kilometres (2 to 2.5 miles) below the surface. Magma, water and gas combine, and heat generates pressure. The magma is then pushed up through the vent toward the crater.

ASH CLOUD
Often when a volcano is active a plume of smoke can be seen coming out of the crater. If the volcano erupts, that plume expands into a cloud of ashes, gas and vapor that may be visible from kilometres away. It can be very dangerous.

CRATER
The crater, or **mouth**, of a volcano sits at the end of the vent. This is where the magma emerges.

SECONDARY VENTS
A volcano's main vent often branches off into secondary vents caused by **extreme pressure**. These may form cracks on the sides of the volcano where additional magma emerges.

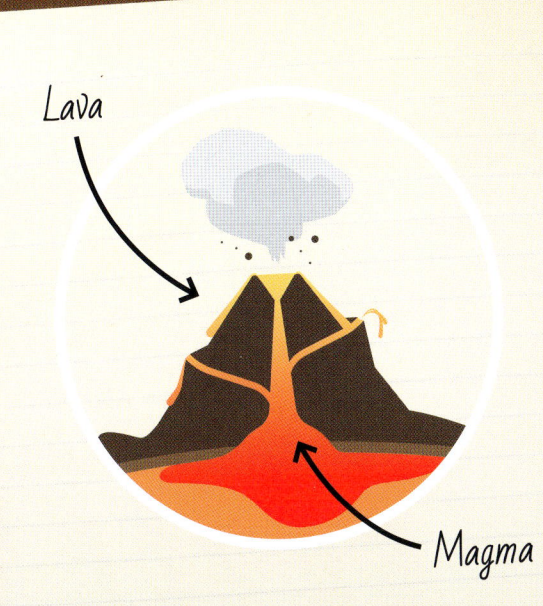

MAGMA OR LAVA?
Magma and lava are related, but they aren't the same thing. Magma is denser and consists of molten rock and gas. Once magma comes out of the crater, it is considered lava. Lava is more liquid and is lighter because it doesn't contain gas.

Lava

Magma

Mount Fuji

A WIDE RANGE

Volcanoes can be categorised in different ways. One way to break them down is by the type of crater. Let's see what types of craters exist.

Stratovolcano

HOW IS THE VOLCANIC EDIFICE FORMED?
A volcano's edifice, meaning its outside structure, is formed by the gradual accumulation of lava and other materials that, eruption by eruption, harden into layers one on top of another.

Shield volcano

IS A VOLCANO ALWAYS CONE-SHAPED?
The shape of a volcano changes depending on the type of eruption and the type of crater. If one central crater erupts, a certain type of structure will form; if a volcano has multiple craters, it will be shaped differently. So, the type of crater is one major factor in a volcano's overall look.

Fissure volcano

Submarine volcano

HOW MANY TYPES OF VOLCANO CRATERS ARE THERE?
Stratovolcanoes and **shield volcanoes** are the two main types of volcano shapes. Both are created over time as material from eruptions is deposited and then hardens.

22

WHAT IS A STRATOVOLCANO?

A stratovolcano is the most eye-catching type of volcano and is shaped in a **perfect cone**. Its sides are steep and travel upward toward the central crater. Stratovolcanoes are fiery mountains formed by many layers, and they are also known as composite cone volcanoes.

WHAT IS A SHIELD VOLCANO?

While a stratovolcano is strikingly tall, a shield volcano is **wide** at the base, with gently sloping sides. A shield volcano resembles a warrior's shield, which is how it got its name. Very thin, fluid lava forms shield volcanoes.

DID YOU KNOW...?

Mount Fuji, in Japan, at 3,776 metres (12,390 feet) in height is the country's tallest mountain. It is also an excellent example of a stratovolcano—and it's still active! One of the most beautiful volcanoes in the world, it is shrouded in mythology and mystery and is considered a sacred place.

Hawaiian Islands

A SHIELD ARCHIPELAGO
The **Hawaiian Islands** are volcanic islands, and most of them are shield volcanoes! **Mauna Loa** is a record-holder. It's the largest of its kind in the world and taller than Everest! It rises more than 5,000 metres (16,400 feet) from the floor of the ocean to the surface of the water, and then there's another portion of almost equal size visible above the water, meaning it's more than 9,000 metres (29,530 feet) tall in total! The tallest volcano, however, is nearby **Mauna Kea**.

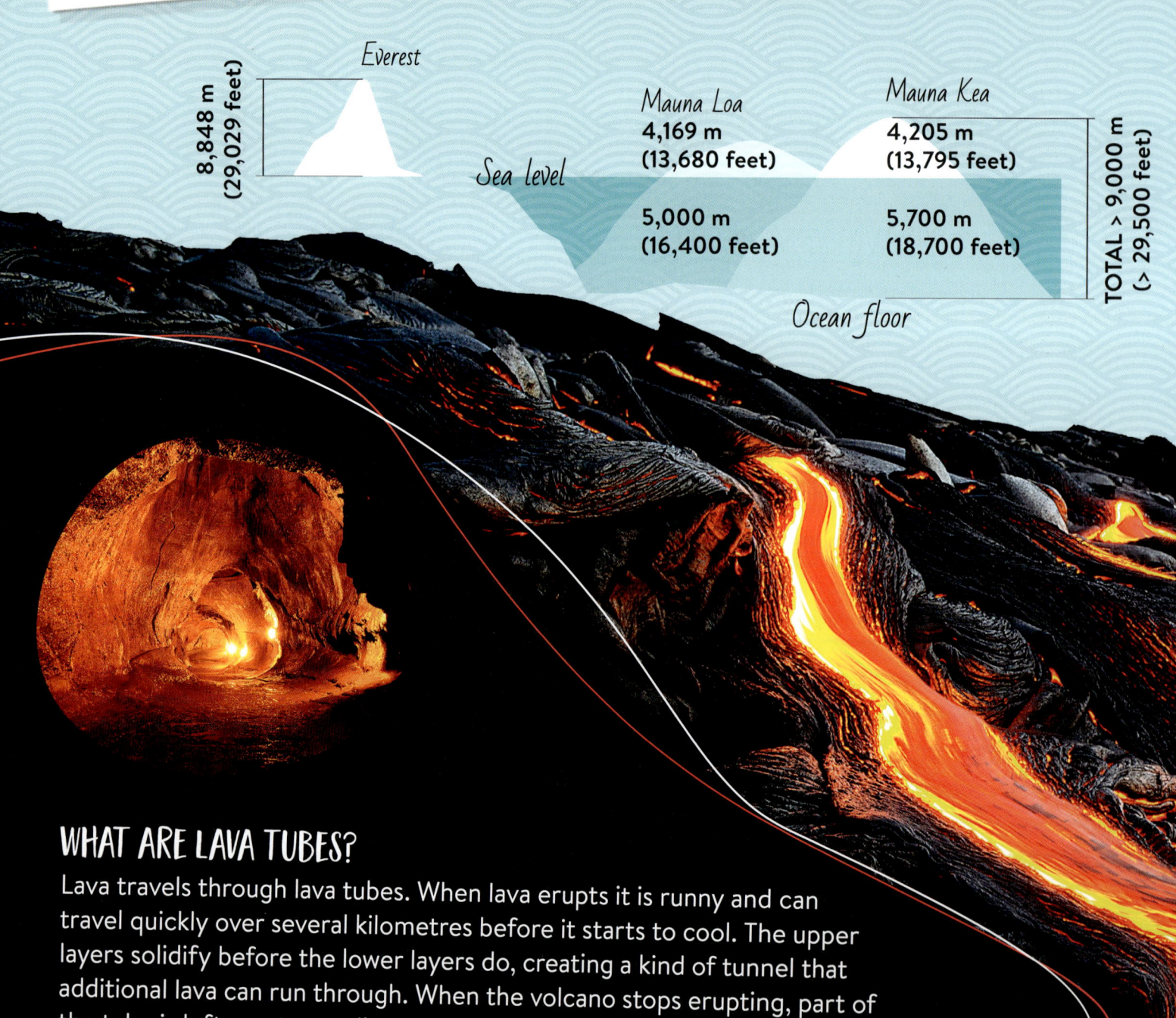

Everest: 8,848 m (29,029 feet)

Mauna Loa: 4,169 m (13,680 feet) above sea level; 5,000 m (16,400 feet) below

Mauna Kea: 4,205 m (13,795 feet) above sea level; 5,700 m (18,700 feet) below

TOTAL > 9,000 m (> 29,500 feet)

Sea level / Ocean floor

WHAT ARE LAVA TUBES?
Lava travels through lava tubes. When lava erupts it is runny and can travel quickly over several kilometres before it starts to cool. The upper layers solidify before the lower layers do, creating a kind of tunnel that additional lava can run through. When the volcano stops erupting, part of the tube is left empty—until next time!

ARE STRATOVOLCANOES AND SHIELD VOLCANOES THE ONLY KINDS OF VOLCANOES?

No, there are also fissure volcanoes and submarine volcanoes.

A **fissure volcano** erupts through a fissure or linear vent in the Earth. These fissures are usually located in spots where plates diverge. Magma collects underneath these cracks and then lava erupts and spreads over the surrounding area.

FISSURE VOLCANO

You may be surprised to learn that **submarine volcanoes**, those located in the depths of the oceans, are the most common volcanoes on the planet. There are 10,000 of them along the mid-ocean ridge! They can erupt very violently.

SUBMARINE VOLCANO

A DISAPPEARING ISLAND

On 7 July 1831 near Sicily in the Mediterranean Sea a small island was spotted. It was the subject of great curiosity. Reports suggest that it was formed due to the eruption of a submarine volcano that created a volcanic cone so high that it stuck out above the surface of the water. The island disappeared a few years later, though, as it was eroded by the elements.

VOLCANO MAP

WHERE CAN VOLCANOES OCCUR?
With a few exceptions, volcanoes tend to form along the borders of **tectonic plates**. Indeed, most of the eruptions on our planet occur in those areas.

HERE'S WHERE YOU'LL FIND VOLCANOES:

- Along **island arcs**, where oceanic plates collide (including volcanoes in Alaska, Japan and Indonesia);

- Along **ocean ridges** (such as the volcanoes in Iceland);

- Along **continental margins**, where an oceanic plate collides with a continental plate and volcanic rock is pushed upward (in North America and the Andes);

- Along **continental rifts**, where new lithosphere is created (in East Africa, for example);

- Near **hotspots** (such as Yellowstone and island archipelagos, including Hawaii, the Canary Islands, the Galapagos, Iceland and Réunion Island).

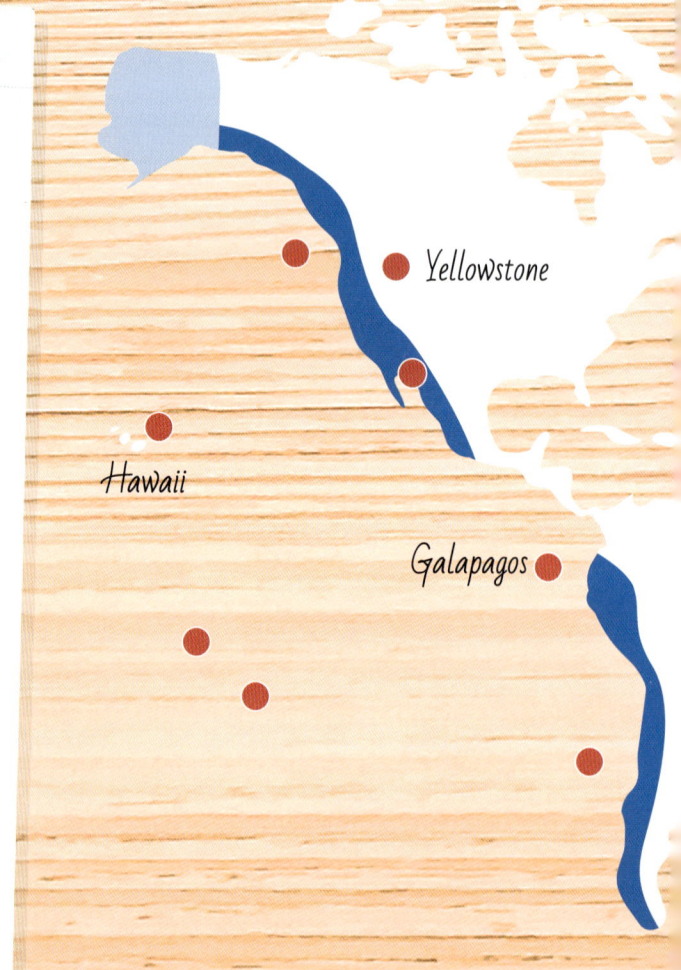

WHAT ARE HOTSPOTS?
Hotspots are areas on the planet where magma rises to the surface directly from deep in the mantle. These hotspots can be far from the borders of plates. Some island chains, such as the **Hawaiian Islands**, are hotspots, and so is **Yellowstone** in the United States.

There are volcanoes in many places on Earth, but as we have learned, they don't occur just anywhere. Another way to categorise volcanoes is to look at them by location and figure out how they are alike or different. Let's explore!

Iceland

Canary Islands

Rift Valley

Réunion Island

Indonesia

WHAT ARE CONTINENTAL RIFTS?

Rifts are deep cracks with smaller branches where magma emerges. They can be dozens of kilometres long, and multiple volcanoes can form along a single rift. One example is the Rift Valley, which runs through several East African countries.

RING OF FIRE

The Ring of Fire around the rim of the Pacific Ocean, also known as the Circum-Pacific Belt, is home to 75% of the volcanic activity on the planet. There are an astonishing number of volcanoes here—more than 400! The Ring of Fire isn't actually ring-shaped but looks more like a **horseshoe**.

ERUPTIONS

Volcanic eruptions are some of the most violent and dangerous natural phenomena, but they are also quite beautiful to see. They occur when magma and other materials are pushed up to the surface of the Earth from far below. Eruptions are unpredictable and can range from gentle to extremely intense depending on a variety of factors.

HOW DOES AN ERUPTION OCCUR?
While each eruption is unique, they do follow certain steps:

1 EARTHQUAKE SWARM
There are almost always warning signs that an eruption is coming. These initial signals include **earthquakes**. An earthquake indicates that a volcano is getting ready to erupt and magma is about to come to the surface!

2 THE ERUPTION ITSELF
An eruption can take the form of a relatively calm lava flow, or it may be a violent explosion, accompanied by clouds of dust, ash, steam and lapilli, or little lava stones. It can even involve **pyroclastic flow**, a dangerous cloud of hot gas.

3 EMANATION
The volcano's eruption is finished. Now the volcano is emitting gas and hot **steam** and quieting down—until it is ready to erupt again.

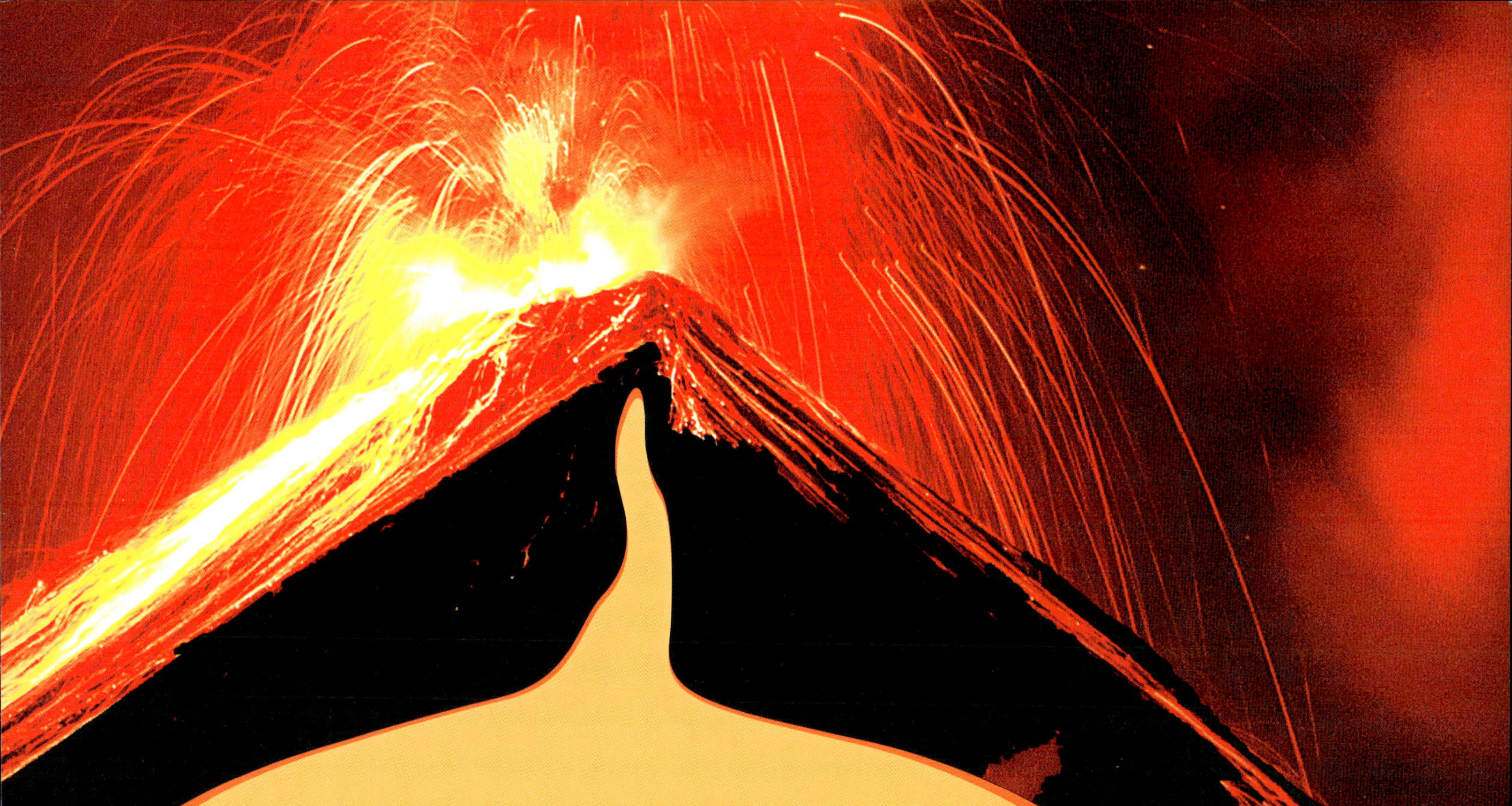

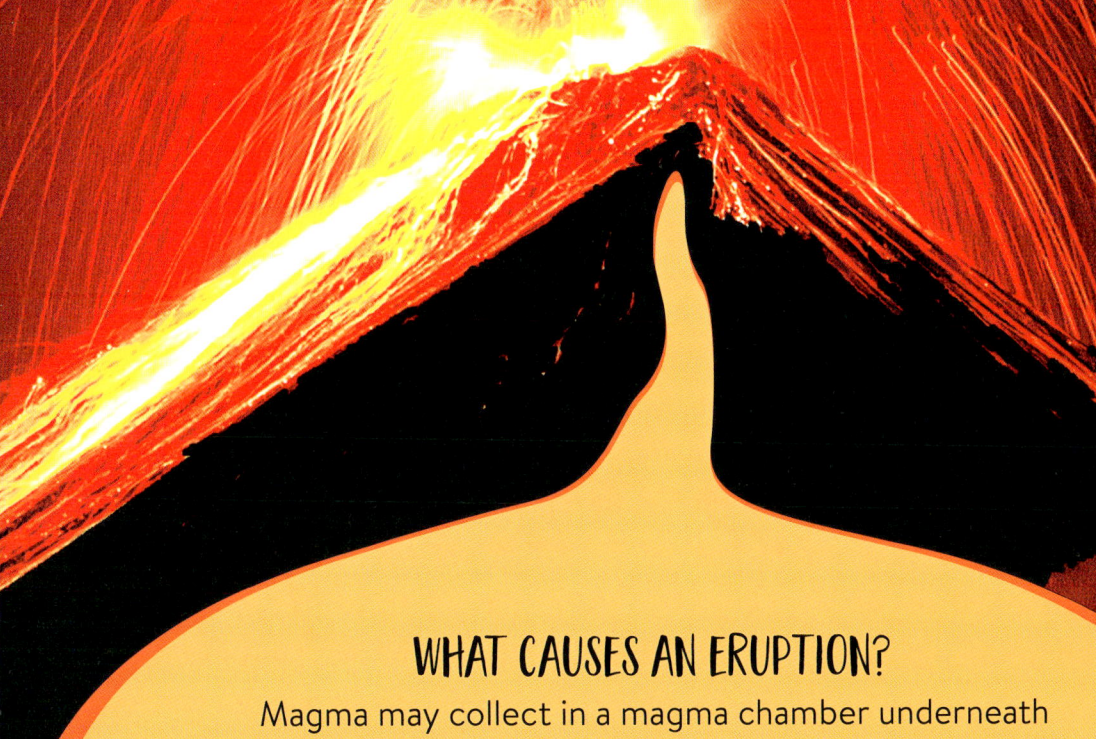

WHAT CAUSES AN ERUPTION?

Magma may collect in a magma chamber underneath the Earth's surface for decades. In optimal conditions, a delicate balance keeps the magma quiet and stable. But it takes only a small change to set an eruption in motion. For example, if the rock below the magma grows weaker or the pressure of the magma builds, an eruption can happen before long.

WARNING SIGNS

Even with modern technology, it's hard to know exactly when a volcano will erupt. There are certain warning signs, however, that an eruption is coming. These can give the inhabitants of surrounding towns and cities a chance to evacuate. These include:

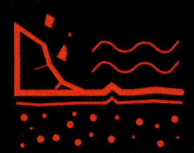

- earthquakes of varying length and intensity;
- changes in the Earth's surface, including cracks; 
- clouds of gas, steam and fumaroles in the soil surrounding the volcano.

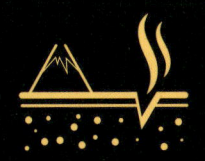

TYPES OF ERUPTIONS

ARE ALL ERUPTIONS THE SAME?
No. Eruptions are usually divided into two categories:

EFFUSIVE ERUPTION
Effusive eruptions push out liquid magma that emerges from the mouth of the volcano and runs down it.

EXPLOSIVE ERUPTION
During an explosive eruption, intense pressure builds inside the volcano. Magma and burning material then shoot forcefully into the air.

CAN AN ERUPTION BE BOTH EFFUSIVE AND EXPLOSIVE?
Yes, it's not uncommon for an eruption to be mixed. Lava flow may combine with explosions.

Volcanoes are very unpredictable!

AN ERUPTION THAT IS MOSTLY EFFUSIVE MAY BE:

Hawaiian eruption: typical of the volcanoes in the Hawaiian Islands, a Hawaiian eruption involves heavy flow of thin, runny lava that solidifies to form a shield volcano.

Icelandic eruption: an Icelandic eruption involves a volcanic fissure or vent—a large crack in the Earth.

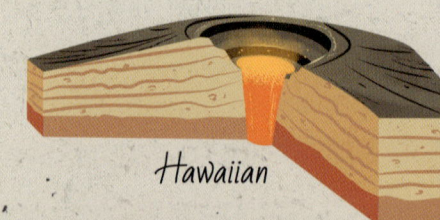

Hawaiian

Icelandic

AN ERUPTION THAT HAS SOME EXPLOSIVE ACTIVITY BUT IS LARGELY EFFUSIVE MAY BE:

Strombolian eruption: these get their name from the Stromboli volcano in the waters off Sicily. Typically, these involve periodic bursts that shoot lava, ash, stones, gas and lapilli hundreds of metres into the air! They also involve lava flow.

Strombolian

A MIXED ERUPTION MAY BE:

Vulcanian eruption: violent explosions produce volcanic 'bombs' and large clouds of gas and ash visible from kilometres away.

Plinian eruption: the most violent eruptions of all, Plinian eruptions are also quite strange; glowing clouds of gas rise high into the air (shaped like pine trees) and then may collapse, forming hot clouds.

Pelean eruption: these destroy the volcanic cone and create burning clouds. Their name comes from the volcano Pelée on the island of Martinique.

Vulcanian

Plinian

Pelean

AN ERUPTION THAT IS EXPLOSIVE ONLY MAY BE:

Hydromagmatic or phreatic eruption: magma comes into contact with water, which turns into steam and causes large explosions that may occur in oceans, lakes or glaciers.

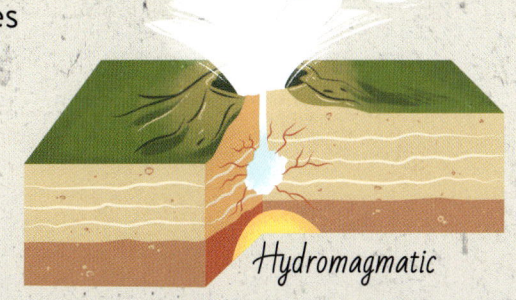

Hydromagmatic

31

EACH ONE UNIQUE

HOW ARE ERUPTIONS CATEGORISED?

The main factors that determine the type of eruption have to do with magma, which is judged for:

viscosity

gas content

water content

Magma is formed by liquids (melted silica, or mineral, compounds); solids (crystals and rocks formed by cooled magma); and gases (carbon dioxide and other gases).

WHAT IS VISCOSITY?

Viscosity is one of the most important characteristics of magma. Magma can be quite viscous or not very viscous at all. Viscosity reflects density and the speed at which something flows. The more silica magma contains, the more slowly it flows.

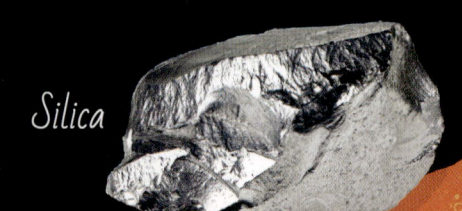

Silica

WHAT EFFECT DO WATER AND GAS HAVE?

The water and gas in magma can change its viscosity. They also can alter the delicate balance of the various components in the magma, which may set off chemical reactions. Those reactions may cause a violent eruption.

Every volcanic eruption is different. How are they categorised? Based on magma!

WHY ARE THESE FACTORS IMPORTANT?

Viscosity (how runny or stiff the magma is) and water and gas content are very important for a number of reasons. If the gas and steam in the magma exert more **pressure** than the liquid it contains and the surrounding rocks can't contain it, or if the magma becomes so dense that it doesn't flow and blocks the mouth of the volcano, the result can be a series of highly dangerous explosive eruptions!

DID YOU KNOW...?

You may have seen images of magma that seems to simmer like a pot of soup. This is due to gas bubbles that form in the magma. Since gas is lighter than magma, they rise to the surface.

LIKE A FIZZY DRINK!

To understand how this phenomenon works, imagine a fizzy drink in a bottle. When the magma moves, the gas separates from the liquid and forms bubbles. As the pressure increases, gas bubbles rise and increase in volume, pushing magma toward the surface. If the gas bubbles have no way to escape, though, like the steam in a magma chamber, they keep growing and eventually explode. The same thing happens if you shake a fizzy drink bottle very hard— eventually the cap pops right off from the pressure!

A DANGEROUS ARSENAL

During an eruption, a volcano emits not just lava, but lots of other rocky and gaseous materials. It's an arsenal of dangerous weapons!

WHAT'S THE TEMPERATURE OF LAVA AND HOW FAST DOES IT FLOW?

When lava rises from the depths of the Earth, it's **incredibly hot**—between 750°C and 1200°C (1380°F and 2190°F)! Once it comes out of the volcano, it cools. As it cools it turns more viscous, so it rarely moves any faster than a few dozen kilometres per hour.

750–1200°C (1380–2190°F)

1–40 km/h (2/3–25 mph)

CAN LAVA FLOW BE STOPPED?

Unfortunately, the answer is no. Though scientists can get close to slow-moving lava and, with the proper precautions, study it carefully, lava cannot be controlled or blocked. It simply flows where it flows and covers everything in its path.

IS ALL LAVA THE SAME?
No, there are various types of lava, categorised by the form it takes once it is solid. The main types of lava are the following:

PAHOEHOE LAVA
Pahoehoe lava flows quickly, so the surface cools off first, while the lava underneath is still very hot. Twisted 'ropes' form on the surface.

PILLOW LAVA
Pillow lava is the most common type of lava and the type emitted by underwater volcanoes. It cools quickly and is very hard.

AA LAVA
Aa is a Hawaiian word meaning 'stone you cannot walk upon'. This type of lava hardens into large, thick blocks.

DID YOU KNOW...?
The colour of lava indicates its temperature: yellow lava is the hottest, while orange and red are cooler—but by no means cold.

VOLCANIC FOAM!
The **Ol Doinyo Lengai** volcano in Tanzania is known for its unusual lava. Its lava is cooler than average (500–600°C, or 930–1110°F) and immediately after an eruption it resembles mud, but as soon as it begins to cool down it turns white so that it looks like foam! The colour is due to the elements making up this unusual type of lava.

Lava rich in sodium carbonate

All solids produced during an eruption are known as **pyroclastic material**. This word comes from the Greek:

pyr (fire) + klastos (broken) = fire fragments

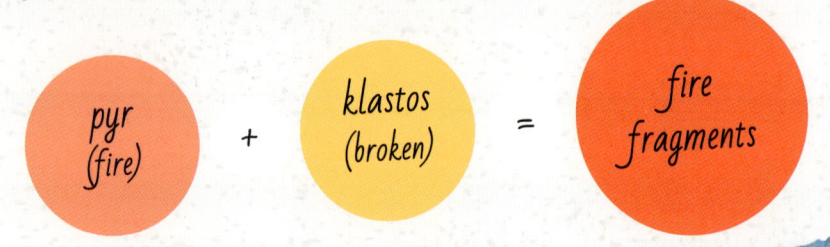

VOLCANIC BOMBS!

During an eruption, a volcano may shoot fragments of lava into the air that cool off before they hit the ground. Such projectiles that measure anywhere from a few centimetres to the size of an automobile are known as volcanic bombs. They are rounded and can even explode in flight due to the pressure generated by the gas trapped inside them.

Bomb

Pyroclastic cloud

1000°C (1830°F)

700 km/h (435 mph)

WHAT IS A PYROCLASTIC CLOUD?

A pyroclastic cloud may form when a volcano erupts. These enormous **red-hot clouds** are formed of gas and other magmatic material and hover over a large area around the volcano.

They are quite dangerous, with temperatures up to 1000°C (1830°F), and they move at top speed—up to 700 kilometres (435 miles) per hour!

Thunder and lightning

THUNDER, LIGHTNING AND LAPILLI!

Lapilli

A volcanic eruption can look truly apocalyptic. Not only are there explosions and lava flows, but static electricity also generates thunder and lightning. Volcanic bombs shoot into the air, accompanied by **lapilli**, smaller pieces of pyroclastic material.

Ash

WHY IS VOLCANIC ASH DANGEROUS?

Volcanic ash is also considered pyroclastic, and during an eruption a volcano makes a lot of it. These tiny particles may seem harmless, but they can cause a lot of damage. If enough ash accumulates, its weight may even cause buildings to collapse. Ash also pollutes water—making it unsafe to drink—and the air. Ash makes roads unusable and is very difficult to remove.

A BRIEF HISTORY OF VOLCANOES

ERUPTIONS TO REMEMBER!

Many volcanic eruptions have changed the course of history, and we have descriptions of them dating back millennia. Here are some of the most catastrophic historic eruptions.

Island of Thera (now Santorini) before and after the eruption.

1500 B.C.E.

THERA, GREECE

More than 3,000 years ago, the Greek island of Thera, now known as **Santorini**, experienced one of the most catastrophic eruptions in history. Massive earthquakes preceded the gigantic explosion and Plinian eruption. The resulting ash covered the island's towns and villages. The eruption also set off a tsunami that reached as far as the island of Crete, more than 100 kilometres (62 miles) away!

79 C.E.

VESUVIUS, ITALY

Vesuvius erupted on 24 and 25 August and killed more than 10,000 people. Initially, there were explosions, and a column of gas and ash rose 15 kilometres (more than 9 miles) into the air. The following day the eruption grew even worse. A lethal cloud formed and shrouded the cities of **Pompeii**, Herculaneum and Stabiae. Ash rained down on these cities, preserving them for centuries.

MODERN FOSSILS

A few decades after ancient Pompeii was excavated, archaeologists began to discover the remains of people and animals preserved inside voids that formed amidst hardened volcanic debris. They created casts that reproduced the victims as they appeared in their tragic final moments.

10,000 deaths

1815

TAMBORA, INDONESIA

This volcano on the island of Sumbawa, in **Indonesia**, saw the worst eruption in recent history with the highest recorded death toll. It caused a giant explosion and a tsunami, and millions of tons of ash were expelled into the atmosphere. The ash even blocked the sun, causing the entire planet to grow colder, which led to famine and even more deaths.

200,000 deaths

1883

KRAKATOA, INDONESIA

On 27 August, volcanoes on the Indonesian island of **Krakatoa** exploded and much of the island collapsed. The loud boom caused by the explosions could be heard up to 3,000 kilometres (more than 1,800 miles) away—as far away as Africa! The resulting cloud rose 80 kilometres (nearly 50 miles) in the air and waves along the coastline were up to 40 metres (130 feet) tall. A few decades later, a new island, Anak Krakatoa, emerged on the spot.

36,000 deaths

1980

57 deaths

MOUNT SAINT HELENS, UNITED STATES

On 18 May in **Washington state** a truly spectacular and frightening eruption occurred. First there were a series of seismic tremors, and then the eruption got underway. It caused a landslide, and one entire side of the volcano slid downward as the volcano erupted. The glaciers at the summit of the volcano melted, causing massive mudslides.

CAPTURED ON FILM

A few weeks before the eruption, photojournalist Reid Blackburn took shots of the volcano. Blackburn then died during the eruption, and the film was forgotten for decades. When it was discovered, it was developed, revealing new images of the volcano just before it changed forever.

VOLCANOES TODAY

Even in the modern era, when we have so many methods for monitoring them, volcanoes can surprise us. Many are under tight surveillance, because they might wake up at any time and threaten the people who live nearby. Here are profiles of some of the most closely watched volcanoes today.

Name:
VESUVIUS

Location:
Naples, Italy

Last eruption:
1944

Why is it dangerous?
The volcano is currently quiet, but it might awaken at any moment. It is also located in Naples, the most densely populated city in Europe, so it's important to anticipate any activity for safety's sake.

ARE THERE CONTINENTS WITHOUT VOLCANOES ON THEM?
No, every continent has at least one or two active volcanoes.

FIRE AND ICE
It might sound funny, but there are even volcanoes amidst the perennial ice of Antarctica. Erebus, located on Ross Island, is 3,800 metres (12,470 feet) tall.

42

Name:
MOUNT RAINIER

Location:
Seattle, Washington, United States

Last eruption:
1894

Why is it dangerous?
Mount Rainier last erupted more than a century ago, but there is a risk that the volcano will awaken and not only experience explosive eruptions but also cause mudslides and debris flow because it has a glacier at its peak.

Name:
GALERAS

Location:
Pasto, Colombia

Last eruption:
2010

Why is it dangerous?
This is Colombia's most active volcano, and it's located near densely populated Pasto. For that reason, this is a volcano to watch. In 1993, an explosion killed three scientists who were surveying the crater.

Name:
NYIRAGONGO

Location:
Goma,
Democratic Republic of the Congo

Last eruption
2021

Why is it dangerous?
There is a permanent lava lake inside this volcano that is 200 metres (more than 650 feet) wide. If that lava were to come out of Nyiragongo, it would result in a massive lava flow. That's what happened in 2002 and again during an eruption in 2021.

Name:
MERAPI

Location:
Java, Indonesia

Last eruption
2021

Why is it dangerous?
This is one of the most active volcanoes in Indonesia and is constantly erupting. The major threat is that lethal pyroclastic clouds could form. That would make it difficult to evacuate the 24 million people who live in the area.

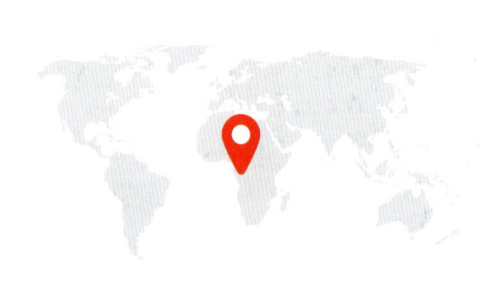

DID YOU KNOW...?
Indonesia is the country with the largest number of active volcanoes: 76!

Name:
PINATUBO

Location:
Manila, Philippines

Last eruption
1991

Why is it dangerous?
This volcano's most recent eruption in 1991 was one of the most violent of the twentieth century. Not only did the volcanic explosion cause great damage, but there was a typhoon as well. Everything in a radius of a few kilometres was wiped away, and it took years to rebuild. As you might imagine, this volcano is closely monitored for any further activity.

Name:
SAKURAJIMA

Location:
Kagoshima, Japan

Last eruption
2021

Why is it dangerous?
This volcano is famous for its violent Plinian and Strombolian eruptions. It's known as the Vesuvius of the East because it resembles the Naples volcano. Because of its recent activity it is closely watched, and preparations have been made: shelters were built in areas around the city so that citizens can evacuate quickly if necessary.

BEYOND FIRE

EARTHQUAKES

Volcanic eruptions have far-reaching effects. Though fiery lava may be contained to the surrounding area, other natural disasters cause additional damage. There is a domino effect as volcanic eruptions disrupt the Earth and the oceans.

WHAT IS AN EARTHQUAKE?
The Earth's outer layer is always moving slowly, but sometimes when two plates move abruptly the energy created makes what are known as **seismic waves**, which cause an earthquake. Sometimes an earthquake is caused by magma moving below the surface during or after an eruption.

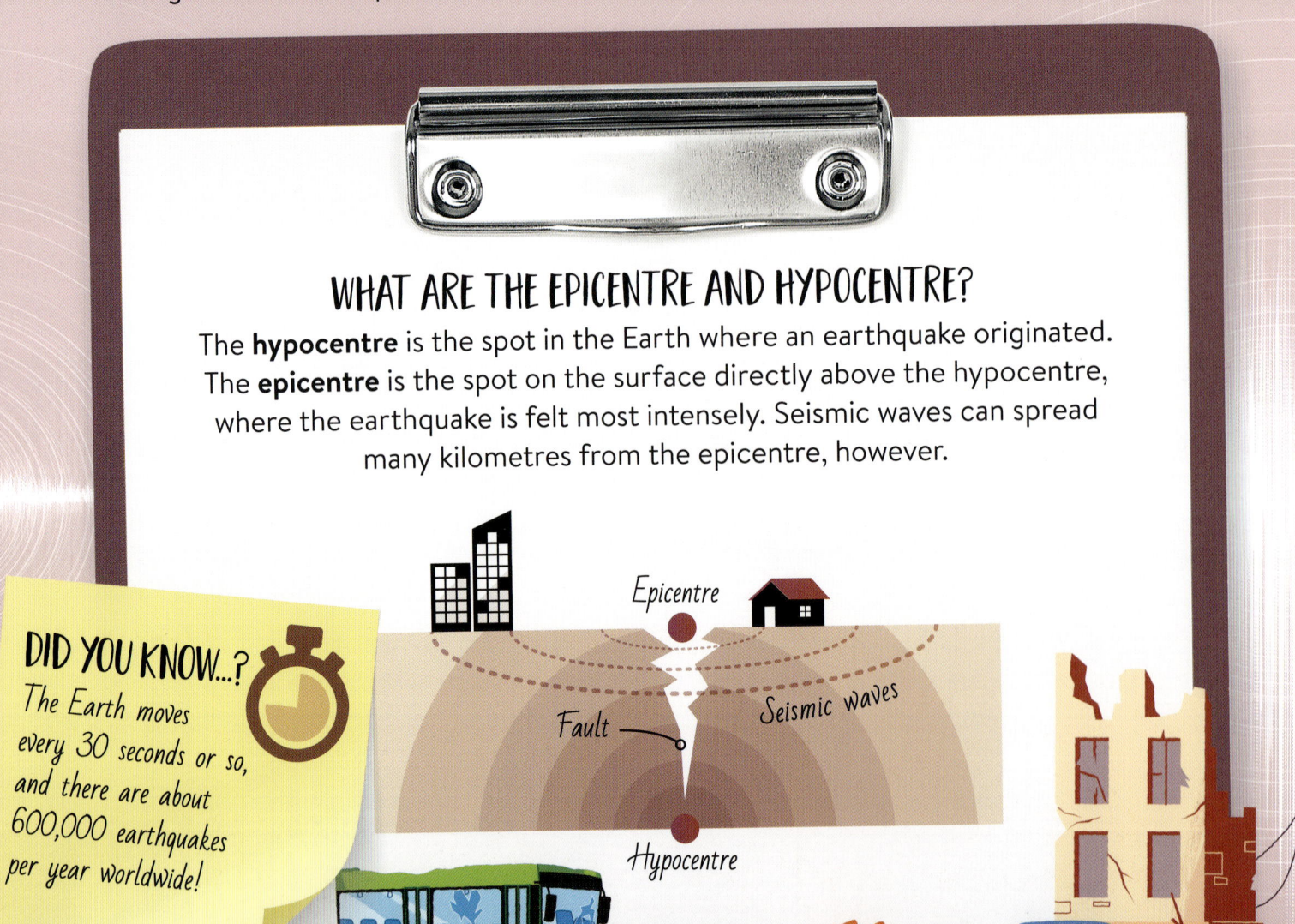

WHAT ARE THE EPICENTRE AND HYPOCENTRE?
The **hypocentre** is the spot in the Earth where an earthquake originated. The **epicentre** is the spot on the surface directly above the hypocentre, where the earthquake is felt most intensely. Seismic waves can spread many kilometres from the epicentre, however.

Epicentre
Fault
Seismic waves
Hypocentre

DID YOU KNOW...?
The Earth moves every 30 seconds or so, and there are about 600,000 earthquakes per year worldwide!

46

IS THE RISK HIGHER IN CERTAIN AREAS?
Like volcanic eruptions, earthquakes happen more often along fault lines and in subduction zones along the edges of lithospheric plates. Areas such as Japan, parts of the western United States, Latin America and some parts of Europe are more prone to earthquakes.

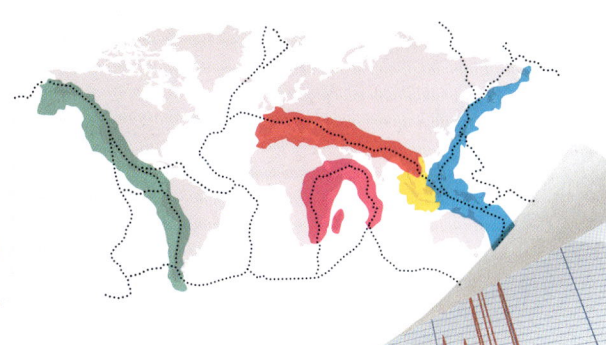

HOW ARE EARTHQUAKES MEASURED?
Tremors are monitored and recorded using several different instruments. A **seismometer** measures a tremor and identifies its source, while a **seismograph** records it.

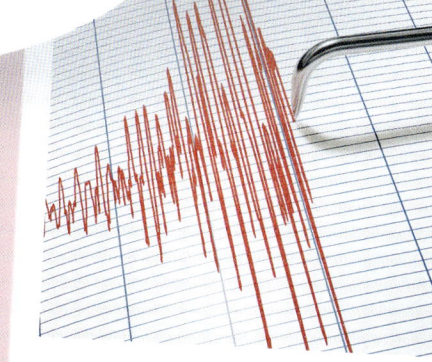

HOW ARE EARTHQUAKES CATEGORISED?
There are two systems for rating the strength of an earthquake: **intensity**, meaning the damage caused to buildings and other items, and **magnitude**, meaning the reach of the seismic waves generated by energy during the seismic event.

They use two different scales:

Mercalli Scale → from 1 to 12
(degrees of intensity)

Richter Scale → from 1 to 10
(degrees of magnitude)

DID YOU KNOW...?
The highest magnitude ever recorded was 9.5 for an earthquake in Chile.

TSUNAMIS

WHAT IS A TSUNAMI?
A tsunami is an exceptionally tall and powerful wave. It forms out in the open sea after an event that generates a lot of energy (an earthquake, a landslide or a volcanic explosion or eruption). These waves have devastating effects on the coast and the mainland once they reach shore.

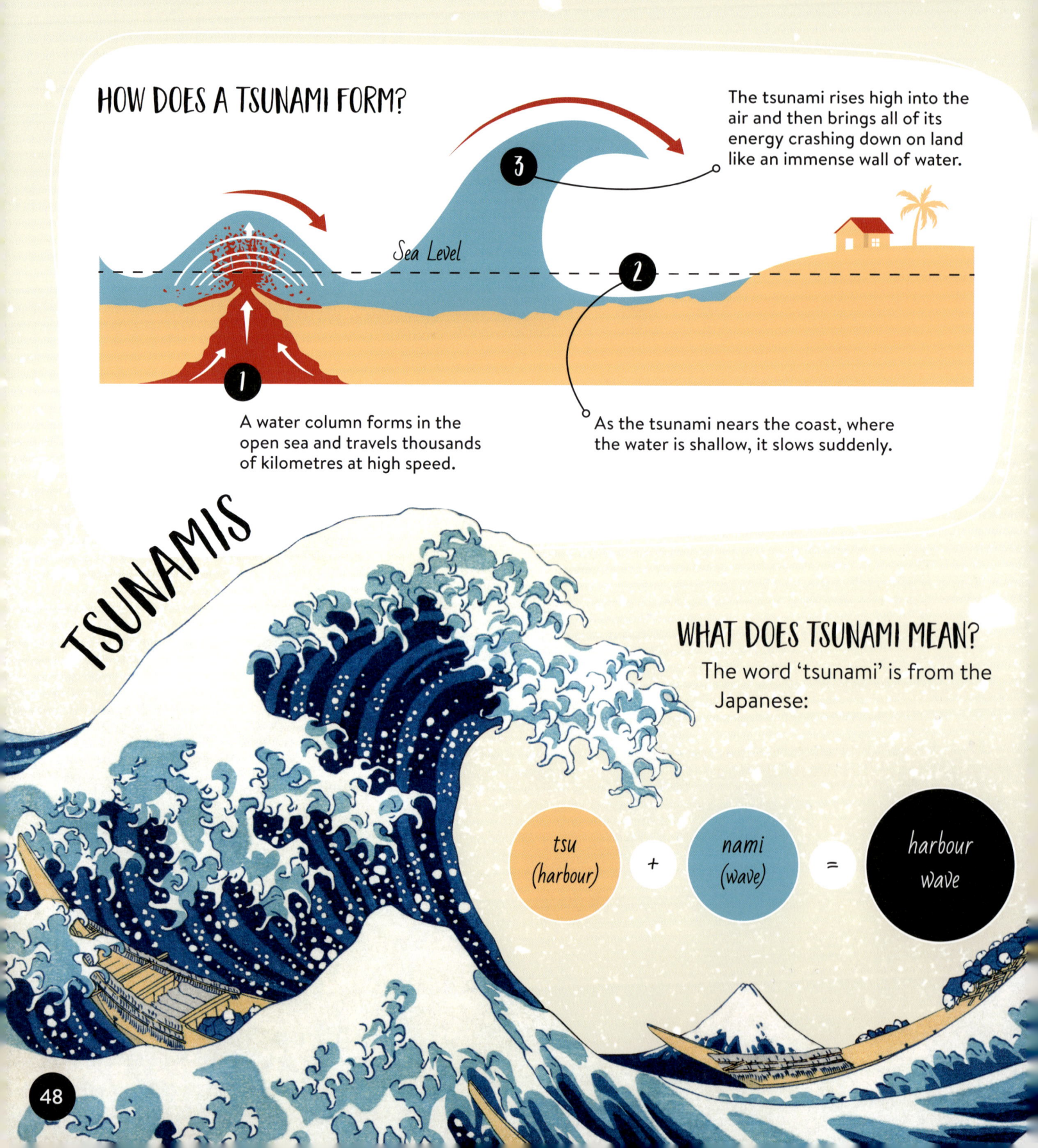

HOW DOES A TSUNAMI FORM?

Sea Level

1. A water column forms in the open sea and travels thousands of kilometres at high speed.

2. As the tsunami nears the coast, where the water is shallow, it slows suddenly.

3. The tsunami rises high into the air and then brings all of its energy crashing down on land like an immense wall of water.

WHAT DOES TSUNAMI MEAN?
The word 'tsunami' is from the Japanese:

tsu (harbour) + nami (wave) = harbour wave

WHERE DO TSUNAMIS FORM?

Tsunamis occur most often in the Pacific Ocean, around the Ring of Fire and in the Indian Ocean. However, there have been some in the Atlantic Ocean and even in the Mediterranean Sea.

CAN YOU ESCAPE A TSUNAMI?

Escaping a tsunami is difficult, because nothing can stop it. But many areas where earthquakes and eruptions are common and often result in tsunamis have been equipped with warning systems to alert the population to imminent danger so they can move further inland to safety.

WHAT WAS THE HIGHEST WAVE EVER?

Tsunamis are difficult to measure, but the highest wave ever is believed to have risen 60 metres (200 feet) into the air!

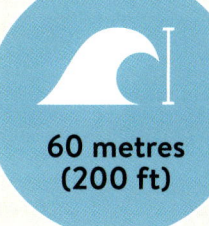

60 metres (200 ft)

800 km/h (500 mph)

DID YOU KNOW...?

These waves can move at speeds of up to 800 km/h (500 mph), as fast as a flying plane!

WHICH TSUNAMI CAUSED THE MOST DAMAGE?

Some recent tsunamis have been truly devastating. The 2004 tsunami in Southeast Asia and one that hit Japan in 2011 caused 230,000 and 15,703 deaths, respectively, as well as incalculable damage to towns and cities and the areas along and near the coasts. The 2004 tsunami was so powerful that it shifted the Earth's axis!

Japan, Fukushima, 2011

ASH CLOUDS

HOW FAR CAN AN ASH CLOUD TRAVEL?
During an eruption, a volcano can produce enormous amounts of ash. The ash forms clouds that then can rise into the stratosphere, tens of kilometres above the Earth!

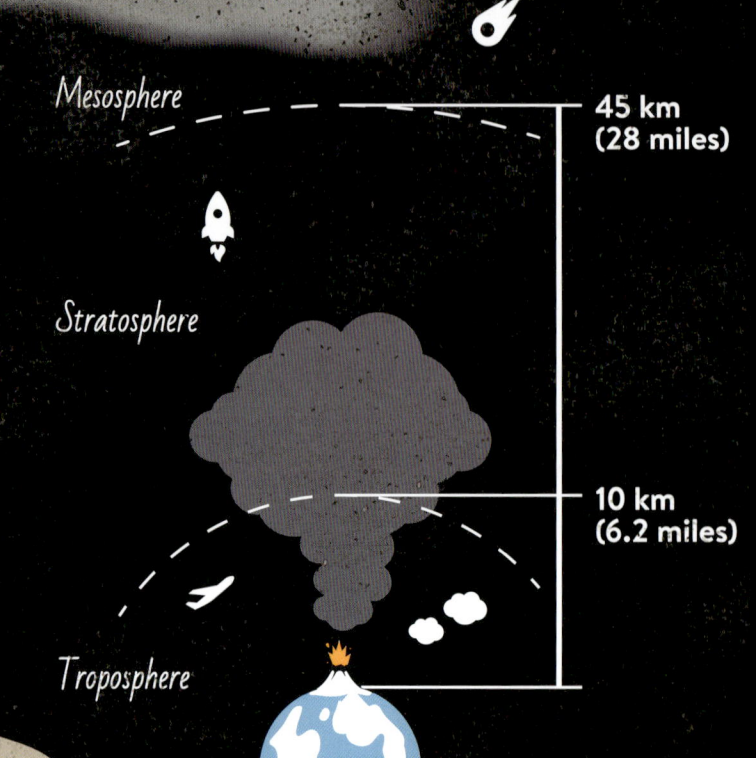

Mesosphere
45 km (28 miles)

Stratosphere

Troposphere
10 km (6.2 miles)

MUDFLOWS

WHAT IS A LAHAR?
A **lahar*** is a dangerous **mudflow** containing pyroclastic materials, ash and other detritus. Like a river overflowing its banks, a lahar runs down the sides of a volcano and overwhelms anyone caught in its path.

WHAT CAUSES A LAHAR?
A lahar can be caused by melting snow and ice that are the result of an eruption. (Often the peaks of volcanoes are covered in snow and even glaciers.) Heavy rains caused by steam from an eruption can also cause a lahar, as can the collapse of a crater under the weight of massive amounts of ash.

*'Lahar' is the Javanese word for lava.

HOW DO ASH CLOUDS AFFECT THE CLIMATE?

Wind can push ash clouds thousands of kilometres from where they formed. They blanket the atmosphere and can cause significant climate change. The **Tambora** eruption in 1815 caused dramatic cooling: the ash caused the Earth's temperature to drop and snow and ice formed during what would typically have been the warm season.

AN ENTIRE CONTINENT GROUNDED

In late spring 2010 an ash cloud from the Icelandic volcano **Eyjafjallajökull** brought European air traffic to a standstill. The ashes were so thick that planes couldn't take off or land until the cloud moved away. Ashes not only block vision but can cause serious damage to plane engines.

WHY ARE MUDFLOWS DANGEROUS?

Mudflows are very dangerous. A mudflow can travel at top speed down the steep slopes of a volcano and bury entire cities, sometimes even in locations dozens of kilometres from the eruption. When the mud dries, it is as solid as cement!

A BURIED CITY

In 1985, a gigantic lahar caused by the eruption of the **Nevado del Ruiz** volcano buried the city of Armeno, in Colombia. The city was covered with 8 metres (26 feet) of mud. More than 23,000 people died.

CALDERAS, GEYSERS AND MORE!

CALDERAS

WHAT IS A CALDERA?
A caldera is an **indentation** in the surface of the Earth with steep sides, basically a large crater. It's no accident that a caldera resembles a volcanic crater: a caldera forms when a volcanic edifice collapses. Shield volcanoes and stratovolcanoes are especially likely to form calderas.

HOW DOES A CALDERA FORM?
A caldera forms as the result of a very intense eruption. Once the magma chamber is empty, it can no longer support the weight of the volcanic edifice. The top of the volcano collapses inward, resulting in a wide crater, or caldera.

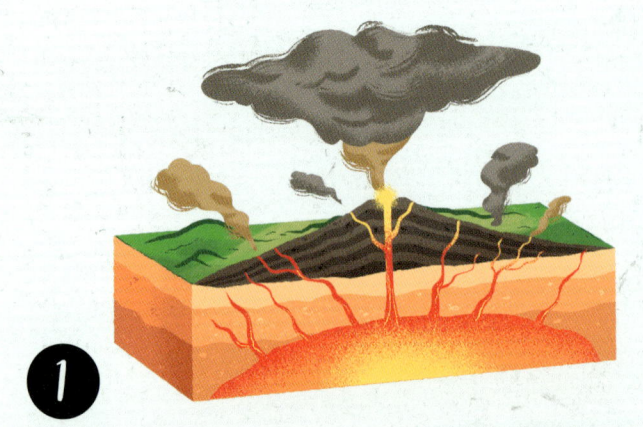

1 Eruption is in full swing: magma rises to the surface through the mouth of the volcano and other openings.

2 Once the eruption has peaked and is beginning to fade, the magma chamber empties out.

3 Without magma, a vacuum forms. The walls of the volcanic edifice collapse and the volcano falls into the magma chamber.

4 A caldera is formed. It may fill with water to become a lake.

A volcanic eruption can be so strong that it destroys the volcano itself. The power of the Earth is felt not only in eruptions, but in other ways as well, some of which may be even more dangerous. Geysers and earthquakes are just some of the potential aftereffects of a volcano.

52–72 KM (32–45 MILES) diameter

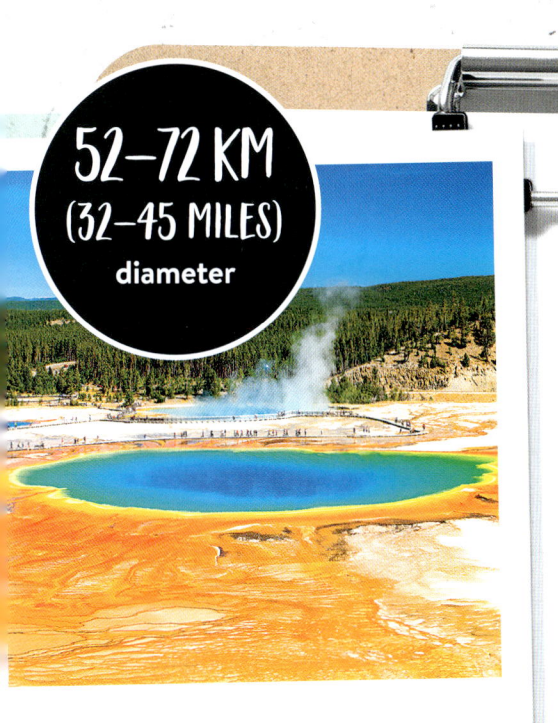

120 KM (74 1/2 MILES) circumference

WHAT'S THE WORLD'S LARGEST CALDERA?

Calderas can be very large and on average are more than 5 kilometres (3 miles) in diameter.

The largest caldera in the world is the Yellowstone Caldera in the United States.

The Mount Aso caldera in Japan is also very large, with a circumference of 120 kilometres (74 1/2 miles)!

Yellowstone, United States

Aso, Japan

WHAT'S A VOLCANIC LAKE?

If a volcano is quiet or extinct, its caldera may fill with water, forming a lake. Some of the world's prettiest volcanic lakes, also known as crater lakes, are in **Kelimutu** in Indonesia. This volcano is home to three different lakes, each a different colour. The volcano could erupt at any moment, however, and those beautiful lakes will quickly turn into dangerous lahars.

SECONDARY VOLCANISM

WHAT IS SECONDARY VOLCANISM?
Secondary volcanism includes all the activity of a volcano that is not actively erupting, such as **vents** and **fumaroles** which emit sulphur and steam mixed with other gases, and **geysers** that shoot out jets of steam.

WHAT IS BRADYSEISM?
Bradyseism is a phenomenon in some areas of the Earth that causes the surface to rise and lower temporarily. No one is sure what causes these movements, but the belief is that they are caused by aquifers under the surface whose water turns to steam from the heat of surrounding magma and rocks. The steam is so plentiful that it alters the stability of the land around it.

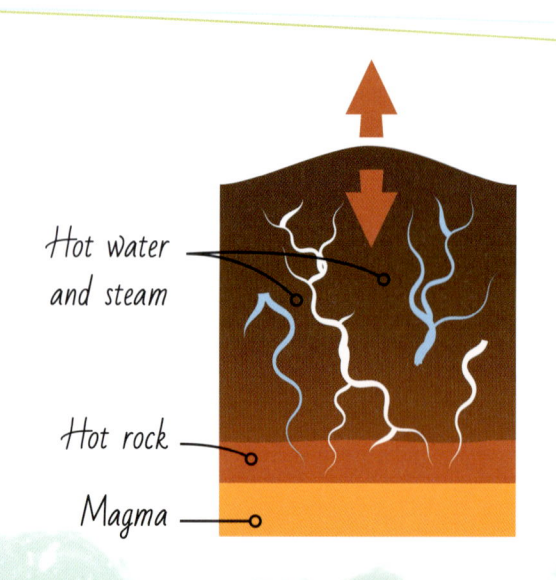

Hot water and steam

Hot rock

Magma

PHLEGRAEAN FIELDS
The **Phlegraean Fields** near Naples, Italy, are the most famous example of this effect. The surface here is quite active, and the phenomenon is linked to the nearby volcano Vesuvius. Basically, this is a large volcanic area that has the potential to explode forcefully.

54

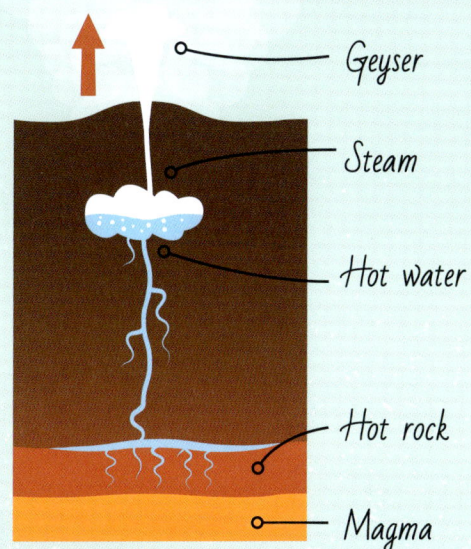

GEYSERS

- Geyser
- Steam
- Hot water
- Hot rock
- Magma

DID YOU KNOW...?
The word geyser comes from Geysir, the name of Iceland's most famous geyser.

WHAT IS A GEYSER?
A geyser is a hot spring that shoots boiling water into the air, often quite high, from the depths of the Earth. This happens when an aquifer and hot rocks meet and form large amounts of steam.

> 100 metres (328 feet)

The world's most famous geyser is **Steamboat** Geyser in Yellowstone Park. It shoots water more than 100 metres (330 feet) into the air.

Other geysers erupt surprisingly regularly, like the Icelandic geyser **Strokkur**, that goes off every 6 to 8 minutes exactly.

6-8 minutes

WHAT IS A SUPERVOLCANO?
A supervolcano is an enormous caldera that would cause tremendous damage to the planet if it erupted. The Yellowstone Caldera and the Phlegraean Fields are both considered supervolcanoes.

STUDYING VOLCANOES

Volcanoes were once a complete mystery. People were at a loss to predict when they would erupt and, understandably, lived in fear of these fiery giants. Today we are lucky that scientific developments allow us to monitor volcanoes. By keeping a close watch on them and recording the warning signs, we can avoid the loss of human life.

MYTHS AND LEGENDS

Before the dawn of modern science, it was basically impossible to predict a volcanic eruption—or to explain why one happened when it did. Many myths and legends developed around these mystical mountains. Some people believed that erupting volcanoes were a sign that the gods were angry. Ancients in Greece, Central America and Northern Europe told tales of supernatural beings that caused volcanoes to erupt.

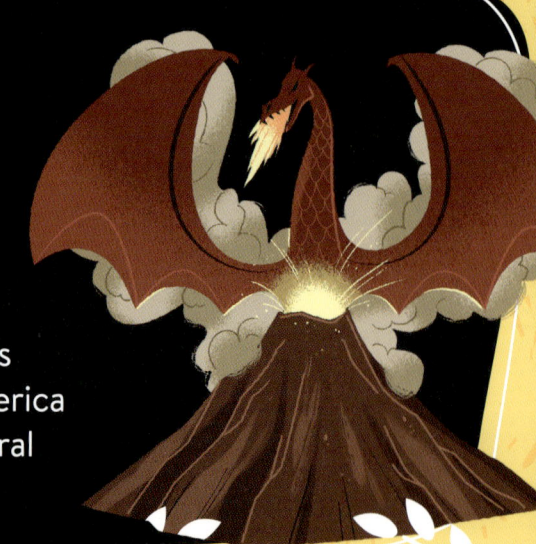

WHAT IS VOLCANOLOGY?

Over time, observers noticed that certain phenomena were linked to volcanic eruptions. They began to piece the puzzle together and founded the science of **volcanology**, which studies volcanoes and related events.

DID YOU KNOW...?
The first volcanologist in history was Pliny the Younger, who documented the eruption of Vesuvius in 79 C.E.

WHAT IS A VOLCANOLOGIST?

A volcanologist is a scientist who studies volcanology. Volcanologists know a lot about the planet and its dynamics. They are familiar with physics, chemistry and geology, all of which are indispensable to understanding volcanoes.

HOW ARE VOLCANOES STUDIED?

Volcanoes are studied both in the laboratory and in the field. In the laboratory, volcanologists look at data and information and analyse samples. They may also simulate eruptions. In the field they observe volcanoes up close—though they always take adequate precautions!

VOLCANOLOGY EQUIPMENT

Volcanologists must protect themselves from heat, because often they are quite close to red-hot lava during an eruption. A volcanologist always has:

- helmet
- gas mask
- gloves and heat-resistant hood
- metal rod
- drone to take video and photos from a safe distance
- pyrometer to measure the temperature of the lava
- fire retardant suit and boots

HOW ARE VOLCANOES MONITORED?

A team of observers and monitoring centres around the world keeps an eye on the most volatile volcanoes and sounds the alarm before an imminent eruption. Additionally, thanks to a satellite network that covers the entire planet, volcanoes can be observed from many different angles so that even the slightest indication of eruption is noted.

A VOLCANO IN THE NEIGHBOURHOOD

You might be wondering how people manage to live around volcanoes when they are so volatile and dangerous. All over the world there are towns, cities and entire nations that have learned to live in harmony with volcanoes—and even to use them to their advantage. Let's look at a few examples.

WHY WOULD ANYONE LIVE NEAR A VOLCANO?

This may sound paradoxical, but the areas around volcanoes have been inhabited since ancient times. It's easy to understand why: the soil impacted by eruptions is **extremely fertile** and ideal for farming. All the materials that emerge from an erupting volcano are rich in minerals and make the soil perfect for growing all sorts of crops. It makes the risk worthwhile!

WHAT IS GEOTHERMAL ENERGY?

The nation of Iceland has harnessed energy from deep underground, known as **geothermal energy**, to meet its needs. Winters are cold in Iceland, and this geothermal energy is used to heat homes, greenhouses and public places and to produce electricity.

ARE VOLCANIC ERUPTIONS USEFUL?

Yes. Eruptions may be devastating, but despite the damage they wreak they may also have some positive results. The rocks and other materials that form when lava cools have been used in everything from construction to sculpture since ancient times. **Basalt** (a very hard rock), **tufa**, **pumice**, **sulphur** and even **diamonds** may be produced by volcanoes, and man has learned to use them all.

Basalt *Tufa* *Pumice* *Sulphur* *Diamond*

PREVENTION IS KEY!

Making an evacuation plan and teaching people what to do when an eruption does occur are very important. In Japan, a country with a great amount of seismic activity and therefore under threat of eruptions and tsunamis, careful preparations have been made and the population is trained to deal with natural disasters. There are signs all over the country with instructions, so no matter what happens, citizens always know what to do and where to go to seek shelter if necessary.

WHAT FEEDS THERMAL SPRINGS?

Countries like Iceland that have many volcanoes also have large numbers of **thermal springs**, also known as hot springs. These are bodies of warm water, and they are the result of geothermal heat. Magma under the surface heats up the surrounding rock, which in turn warms the water.

At Iceland's Blue Lagoon, the water is warm enough to swim comfortably in the dead of winter!

59

IT'S YOUR TURN!

Be sure to ask an adult for help!

Use all the fun facts you've learned to make your own erupting volcano!

CREATE AN ERUPTION!

Follow the instructions below to create a volcanic eruption in the safety of your own home. Let's get started!

To make the volcano you'll need:

| sheet of black paper |  compass |  scissors |  adhesive tape |

To make it erupt you'll need:

| tray or platter |  cardboard box |  glass jar |  bicarbonate of soda |

| pitcher |  dish soap |  white wine vinegar |  red tempera paint |

1 To make the volcano, use a compass to draw two concentric semicircles on the black paper, one large and one small. Cut around the larger semicircle and tape the ends of each line together to form a cone. Use adhesive tape to join the edges.

2 Place the cardboard box on top of the tray or platter. Place the glass jar on top of the box. The opening at the top of the jar will be your crater. Place the paper cone over the jar and box.

Keep the height of the box and jar in mind when making your volcano.

3 Pour dish soap into the pitcher and add vinegar. Then add the red tempera paint.

4 Place 2 teaspoons of bicarbonate in the jar. Slowly pour in the mixture from the pitcher.

Wait a few seconds and your volcano will erupt!

61

QUIZ

You've learned lots of fascinating information about volcanoes and other natural phenomena. Can you match each term to its definition*?

Terms	Definitions
TSUNAMI	Jet of hot water that shoots into the air at more or less regular intervals.
RING OF FIRE	An exceptionally large and powerful wave caused by an earthquake or volcanic eruption.
GEYSER	Theory that explains why the continents exist in their current locations.
VOLCANO	Rift in the Earth's crust where magma escapes, sometimes in violent fashion.
CONTINENTAL DRIFT	A cloud of hot gas that forms as a result of an explosive eruption.
PYROCLASTIC CLOUD	An area around the Pacific Ocean with a very high number of volcanoes.

*You'll find all the definitions in this book!

FIND THE VOLCANOES

Our planet is dotted with volcanoes. Can you match each volcano on the list with its correct location on the map?

| Mount Saint Helens | Pinatubo | Vesuvius | Eyjafjallajökull | Galeras | Mount Fuji | Nyiragongo |

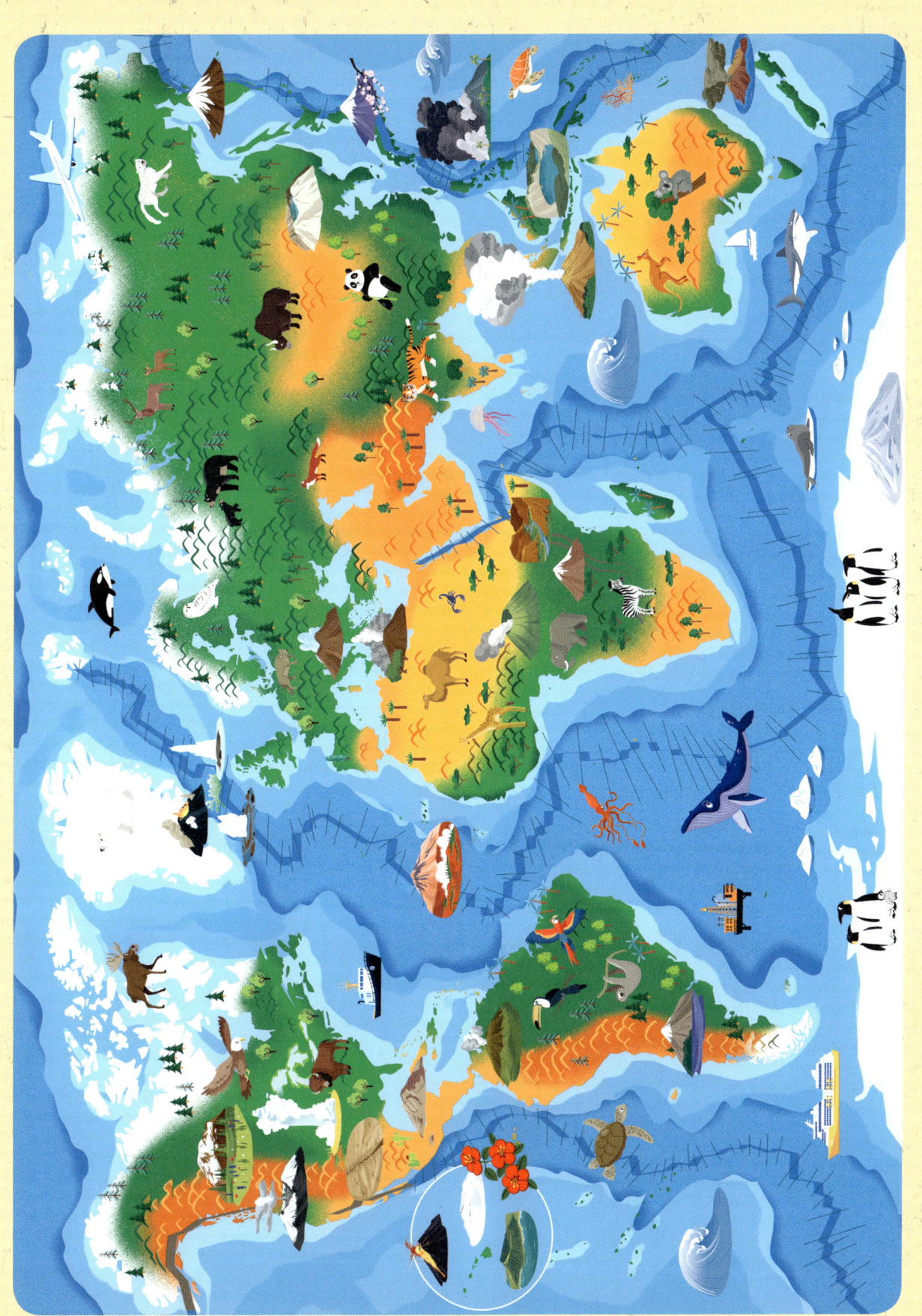

*You'll find all volcanoes in this book!

SASSI

© 2021 Sassi Editore Srl
Viale Roma 122/b
36015 Schio (VI) - Italy

Text: Valentina Bonaguro
Illustrations: Mattia Cerato
Design: Alberto Borgo
Translation: Natalie Danford

Printed in Italy. All rights reserved.

POSTER
50x70cm (19.7"x27.6")